SACRED CONVICTION

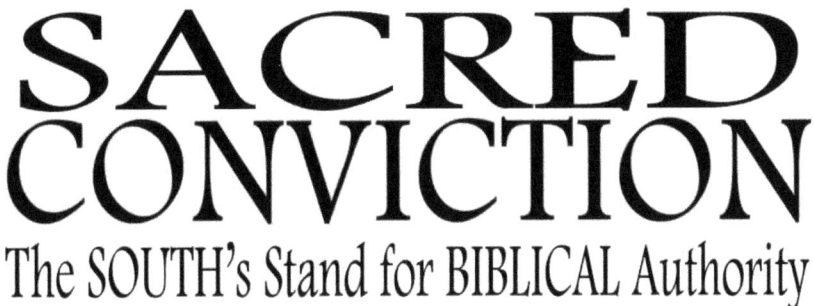

SACRED CONVICTION
The SOUTH's Stand for BIBLICAL Authority

JOSEPH JAY

SHOTWELL PUBLISHING

Columbia, South Carolina

SACRED CONVICTION: THE SOUTH'S STAND FOR BIBLICAL AUTHORITY
Copyright © 2018 by Joseph Jay

ALL RIGHTS RESERVED. No part of this publication may be reproduced, distributed, or transmitted in any form or by any means, including photocopying, recording, or other electronic or mechanical methods, or by any information storage and retrieval system without the prior written permission of the publisher, except in the case of very brief quotations embodied in critical reviews and certain other non-commercial uses permitted by copyright law.

Produced in the Republic of South Carolina by
Shotwell Publishing, LLC
Post Office Box 2592
Columbia, South Carolina 29202

www.ShotwellPublishing.com

Cover Image: Adapted from "Principal church, Charleston," by A. Meyer (1861). Drawing shows men, women and children walking past St. Michael's Episcopal Church in Charleston, SC on the eve of the War. (Courtesy Library of Congress)
Cover Design: Hazel's Dream / Boo Jackson TCB

ISBN-13: 978-1947660106
ISBN-10: 1947660101
10 9 8 7 6 5 4 3 2 1

Contents

Preface ix

Chapter 1: "All [Northern] Ground is Sinking Sand" 1

    Theological Liberalism in the North 3

    Theological Conservatism in the South 6

    The Northern Social Crusade 8

Chapter 2: Slavery In The Christian South 15

    The Middle Passage 16

    Racism and the Perpetuation of Slavery 18

    Plantation Life 22

    Cotton Field Meets Mission Field 25

    The Slave as Human 31

Chapter 3: A Higher Law 35

    Northern Religion and the Protectionist Tariff 37

    Slavery Debated 40

Hath God Said?.. 47

CHAPTER 4: BE YE SEPARATE 53

Religious Politics vs. Political Religion 54

Invasion of the Abolitionists... 57

Denomination Fragmentation 68

CONCLUSION... 78

BIBLIOGRAPHY.. 80

ABOUT THE AUTHOR 89

TO MY FATHER, who gently instilled within me a love for theology and an appreciation for the South.

"The things you have learned and received and heard and seen in me, practice these things, and the God of peace will be with you."
–*Philippians* 4:9 *(New American Standard Bible)*

Preface

THE WAR BETWEEN THE STATES fascinates me. It was, in the truest sense, a clash of cultures, of ideas, and of men. It shaped, and continues to shape, the character of America. Students of history have long experienced the amazing privilege of discovering in great quantity, a rare form of manly character exhibited in the lives of men such as Robert E. Lee, Stonewall Jackson, and Joshua Chamberlain. Biographies of such heroes fill the shelves at local bookstores, as do analyses of the battles they engaged in.

Similarly, a great many historical works have engaged the topic of "cause." What would compel such men of high character (and perhaps sometimes those of not-so-high character) to raise arms against one another? Much ink has been spilled on the constitutionality of secession, the Fugitive Slave Act, protectionist tariffs, and the abolitionist movement. As a result, the conflict is often cast as "the commercial North against the agrarian South," "Puritans against Cavaliers," "centralization against State's rights," and of course "freedom against slavery." In our own day and age, the issue may well be summarized by younger Americans as "equality against inequality." While many of these re-tellings have some truth to them, they tend to ignore one vitally important element—theology.

A. W. Tozer once remarked that, "What comes into our minds when we think about God is the most important thing about us." The narratives of "secular culture against Bible-belt," "humanism against Christianity," or "Reason against Scripture" have largely been ignored. To Christians, this oversight should not come as a surprise. In a materialistic society, events are typically reduced to economic factors in which self-interest and natural law determine cause and effect. Religion is only highlighted if it can be thought of as contributing to materialistic motivations. This, however, is not the way the world works. Material things may be the god of some but let us not assume they are the god of *everyone*. Not everything is reducible to money and power. There are principles, ideals, and God — the passions for which found a much greater level of strength in the consciences of 19th century American men and women.

One of the great tragedies of historical analysis is the failure to account for theological motivations. Northerners and Southerners alike were very religious, though their religions were very different. The North increasingly moved in a humanistic direction, while the South maintained an orthodox Christianity. Southerners were originalists when it came to the founding documents in large part because they were originalists when it came to Scripture. Their political justification for secession upon "State's rights" flowed from this view. Albert Taylor Bledsoe wrote, in what would have been the legal defense of Jefferson Davis had the former president been tried, that "'exegesis,' . . . [does not allow] the preacher to ramble . . . without regard to the real sense of his text." Bledsoe argued, if historical exegesis was applied to the political speeches of New England, "How many splendid orations, and grand soaring flights of rhetoric, will it not spoil . . !" Complimenting this notion is *Ethnogenesis* by Henry Timrod, the poet laureate of the Confederacy. He described the North as having a "religion" but not a "Christian faith." The third verse of his poem, dedicated at the First Confederate Congress, portrayed the North as holding to "creeds that dare to teach, what Christ and Paul refrained to preach," being characterized by "vague philosophies," "fanatic passion," "Pharisaic leaven," and "making laws to stay the laws of heaven."

The economic threat of immediate emancipation without compensation (or integration into the western territories and the North) along with a high tariff certainly served as motivation for the South to disengage. Clearly though, something deeper was also going on. The cartoon of history which says the South only fought "for slavery" transforms into less than a picture of brutish abuse, and more than a mere defense of an economic system when the light of religion is shed upon it. Similarly, "preserving the Union" as a justification for Northern invasion loses the noble patriotic garb and dons the robe of what resembles State-worship, if the "fiery Gospel writ in burnished rows of steel," as *the Battle Hymn of the Republic* refers to it, is examined. When the War Between the States is seen as a theological conflict, a fragmented picture becomes clarified as other "causes" find their proper place within the religious context.

Viewed through these lenses, the question then becomes, "Has the 'Civil War' ever really ended or is it still being fought between a Christian South and a secular North?" The major aim of this short work is simple: to fill in the hole. To answer a question that has not been asked nearly enough. "How did theological differences between the North and South lead to what became 'the Civil War?'" The focus of this book is upon the denominational divisions that took place among the Baptists, Methodists, and Presbyterians immediately preceding and foreshadowing the tragic war.

One more important matter. It should be stated at the outset that no aspect of this work can justify, nor is intended to justify, the American slave labor system. For example, mentioning charitable plantation conditions is not meant to sugar coat the institution. This reality is, however, important to note because it does factor into the actual issue that brought about theological conflict. If, by and large, Christian Southerners were operating according to biblical parameters in how slaves were treated, then their participation could not be considered "sinful" in and of itself.

In recent years an aggressive campaign against Southern heroes and symbols of the 19th century has reached a fever pitch even within historically Southern denominations. As I write this introduction, I am reminded of a proposed submission to the resolutions committee of the Southern Baptist Convention earlier this year which, among other things, denounces the first president of the organization, William B. Johnson, for claiming in "his inaugural address that Southern Baptists were 'free to promote slavery' arguing that slavery was a legal and civil matter, not a church matter." The president of one of the largest Southern Baptist seminaries was a co-sponsor. At a major reformed evangelical conference earlier this year, one of the most influential pastors in the Presbyterian Church of America, who happens to hail from the South, publicly pitched an emotional indictment against "Baptists and Presbyterians" of the "19th century leading up to 1837." Their sin? They allegedly "decided that slavery and slaveholding was dividing the church" so they told themselves that "'If you talk about stuff like that in the church you're getting into politics and social life.' . . . and all the while they were saying [that loving your neighbor] doesn't apply here." This sudden interest in disparaging the denominational founders is driven by current political concerns, not an up-tick in historical interest.

In our modern egalitarian age, political status primarily defines human worth. The thought of any group being deprived in any way of political expression is horrifying. Assumed implicitly is the idea that plantation life was an extension of white supremacy. Even if most masters treated their slaves according to Christian charity and biblical restrictions, their involvement could never be justified from a progressive perspective. Condition is irrelevant so long as status is maintained. Political mobility is more important than general welfare, even if it must come on the heels of economic ruin and cultural destruction, as it did in the aftermath of the War Between the States.

However, before the war, the controversy surrounding slavery centered on condition. Southerners, it was said in travel novels and Northern newspaper features, characteristically mistreated their slaves in the cruelest fashions. Public outrage boiled over on both sides of the debate. Generally speaking, abolitionists were not concerned about the social status of blacks, but they were furious at how slave masters allegedly treated their slaves. With the concurrent rise of New England heresies, abolitionists eventually adopted the idea that relationships between masters and slaves were intrinsically sinful. Masters, and Southerners in general, became quite defensive. To them, this concept was foreign to biblical ethics and subverted scriptural authority.

After the war, former slaves were afforded a political mobility previously unrealized. This new situation increasingly became used as justification for the devastating consequences of the conflict. The progressive paradigm today sees the liberation of man from social and political constraints as the supreme moral good. This good can only be achieved by popular participation in governmental force. This is the main reason the founders of the Southern denominations are vilified. Although they professionally supported charitable treatment of slaves and personally supported progressive emancipation, they did not use their office to compel collectively forcing masters to free their slaves.

Such men are carelessly misrepresented and vilified when subjected to a progressive historical paradigm. The aim of this work is to offer a much different paradigm; one which seeks to fairly represent men of their own time by the light of the Scripture they believed in.

My advice is to read the book in its entirety, stopping along the way if need be to look up original citations for yourself. Much of what you read will probably be new to you. My hope is that this short work will at the very least humanize a class of men who have become reviled without first being understood. While history may not repeat itself exactly, it is and will continue to be cyclical as long as the fallen sons of Adam are the players. If you listen closely to the current voices of many evangelical leaders in America, you may hear the faint whispers of what became the antebellum Northern denominations. Knowing of the disastrous waves these denominations took on the banks of the social gospel - after subsequently giving up on the authority of Scripture - can serve as a warning. Perhaps the Southern denominations can teach us something about current situations facing the church. My greatest prayer is that the Lord uses this work in your life as you gaze upon His unfolding divine plan in history, a plan often forwarded by fallible but ever faithful men whom God still raises up to lead His church - often through what appear to be dark and confusing times.

CHAPTER 1
"ALL [NORTHERN] GROUND IS SINKING SAND"

IN JULY OF 1851 the *Southern Literary Messenger* published portions of an address by the prominent Southern Presbyterian James Henley Thornwell:

> The parties in this conflict are not merely abolitionists and slave-holders – they are atheists, socialists, communists, red republicans, jacobins, on the one side, and the friends of order and regulated freedom on the other. In one word, the world is the battle-ground – Christianity and Atheism the combatants; and the progress of humanity the stake.[1]

Though Thornwell, the "Calhoun of the Southern Church," viewed "the prospect of disunion [with] ... absolute horror," he also knew that "a peaceful dissolution [was] utterly impossible" in an "age of tumults, agitation, and excitement, when socialism, communism, and a rabid mobocracy seem everywhere."[2] Less than

---

[1] Jno. R. Thompson, "Slavery As A Moral Relation," *Southern Literary Messenger* (Richmond, July 1851), XVII , 405.

[2] B.M. Palmer, *The Life and Letters of James Henley Thornwell*, (Richmond: Whittet & Shepperson, 1875), 478-479.

a decade after this prophetic insight, the first official shots were fired in what most Americans know as "The Civil War."

Thornwell's characterization of what did become the War Between the States may sound 160 years too early. Most modern Americans view the mid-1800s as a religious time in the nation's history, not a time when disputes between atheism and Christianity were typical. In one sense this view is correct. As church historian Mark Noll has observed, when comparing the presidential elections of 1860 to 2004, a decrease of between 67 percent and 75 percent in religious involvement among voters can be demonstrated from the former to latter period.[3] Indeed, the war came right off the heels of the Second Great Awakening. Abraham Lincoln himself, though likely not an orthodox Christian – if a Christian at all[4] – famously observed in his second inaugural, "Both [sides] read the same Bible, and pray to the same God."[5] While all this may be true in a broad sense, the majority of Southern churchmen would not have shared Lincoln's sentiment. Both sides may have read the same Bible, but each approached it with a very different method of interpretation. Both sides may have used the same terminology in reference to God, but the conception of Him was not identical. As we shall discover, northerners were by and large atheistic toward the Southern God.

---

[3] Mark Noll, *The Civil War as a Theological Crisis* (Chapel Hill, N.C.: University of North Carolina Press, 2006), 12.

[4] Rondel H. Rumburg, *Was Abraham Lincoln a Christian? A Debate* (Spout Spring: Virginia Society for Biblical and Southern Studies, 2006).

[5] Ronald White, *Lincoln's Greatest Speech: The Second Inaugural.* (New York: Simon & Schuster Paperbacks, 2006), 114.

Theological Liberalism in the North

As late as 1850, the premier Southern statesman John C. Calhoun, in a speech delivered to Congress stated, "The cords that bind the States . . . are [in large part] spiritual or ecclesiastical."[6] Unfortunately, it was the snapping of these cords that eventually led to war. Historical contemporary Rev. A.A. Porter maintained,

> "[The] present revolution is the result of their [the church's] uprising. Much as is due to many of our sagacious and gifted politicians, they could effect nothing until the religious union of the North and South was dissolved, nor until they received the moral support and co-operation of Southern Christians."[7]

Confederate Gen. Thomas R.R. Cobb, a Presbyterian, made the same point in 1862, stating, "This revolution has been accomplished mainly by the churches."[8] Before 1837, when the first of the denominational splits occurred in the Presbyterian church, the widening theological gap was evident. One of the best ways to observe this divergence is by examining the opposite reactions each region had toward the flood of European rationalism and Higher Criticism that washed up on American shores in the 19th century.

---

[6] Richard K. Cralle', *The Works of John C. Calhoun* (New York.: D. Appleton and Company, 1854), 557.

[7] Robert Livingston Stanton, D.D., *The Church and the Rebellion: A Consideration of the Rebellion Against the Government of the United States; and the Agency of the Church, North and South, in Relation Thereto* (New York: Derby & Miller, 1864), 198.

[8] *Ibid.*, 197-198.

The North (especially the Northeast) readily welcomed humanistic ideas in the form of new religions and denominations. Such groups as the Unitarians, Transcendentalists, Quakers, Universalists, and Shakers, as well as utopian schemes such as the Oneida Community and Brook Farm, found fertile soil exclusively north of the Mason-Dixon line. In 1785, King's Chapel in Boston became the first American church to adopt a Unitarian liturgy.[9] It wasn't long until other regional churches followed suit, "Bishop Burgess has said that in 1843 there were one hundred and thirty Unitarian Congregational churches in Massachusetts, hardly twenty of which were Unitarian in their origin."[10] 19th century Unitarian minister George Willis Cooke informs us that:

> Of the period from 1826 to 1832, when Dr. Lyman Beecher father of Harriet Beecher Stowe] was settled in Boston, Mrs. Stowe has given this testimony: 'all the literary men of Massachusetts were Unitarian; all the trustees and professors of Harvard College were Unitarian; all the elite of wealth and fashion crowded Unitarian churches; the judges on the bench were Unitarian.'[11]

---

[9] J.T. Sunderland and Brooke Herford, "The Bi-Centennial of King's Chapel, Boston," *The Unitarian: A Monthly Magazine of Liberal Christianity*, 1887, 4.

[10] Paul E. Lauer, *Church and State in New England*, II-III, 10th Series, (Baltimore: The Johns Hopkins Press, 1892), 188.

[11] G.W. Cooke, *Unitarianism in America: A History of its Origin and Development* (American Unitarian Association, 1902), 384.

Such drastic developments were a result of Enlightenment trends in Europe.[12] Educators like Joseph Stevens Buckminster infiltrated Northern universities, ushering in an era of German Higher Criticism.[13] Harvard University itself went Unitarian with the election of Reverend Henry Ware as Hollis Professor of Divinity in 1805,[14] an event that "not only [made it] the seat of liberalism but also, by necessity, the seat of anti-Calvinism."[15] Even the First Church in Boston, founded by John Winthrop, became Unitarian under the guidance of Jonathan Edwards's opponent, Charles Chauncy. Both Unitarianism and Transcendentalism – which had also become extremely wide-spread[16] – share at their core the belief that man is innately good and morally perfectible through education[17] and social reform. Reason is placed above revelation, with the result being man's devaluation.

After teaching at institutions of higher learning in the North, English-born Unitarian Thomas Cooper became president of South

---

[12] Mark Noll, *A History of Christianity in the United States and Canada* (Grand Rapids, Mich.: Eerdmans, 1992), 98.

[13] Richard Grusin, *Transcendentalist Hermeneutics: Institutional Authority and the Higher Criticism of the Bible* (Durham, N.C.: Duke University Press, 1991), 62.

[14] Sam Blumenfeld, "How Harvard Went from Calvinism to Unitarianism," March 1, 2011.

[15] S.L. Blumenfeld, *Is Public Education Necessary?* (Devin-Adair Co., 1981).

[16] C. Gregg Singer, *A Theological Interpretation of American History*, 2nd ed. (Phillipsburg, N.J.: Presbyterian and Reformed Pub. Co., 1981), 64.

[17] Edward Ayers, "American Passages: *A History of the United States*, 4th ed. (Boston: Wadsworth/Cengage Learning, 2009), 323.

Carolina College in 1821. James Henley Thornwell, who also taught at the institution – eventually succeeding Cooper as president of the college in 1851 – made it a point to oppose Cooper's biblical Higher Criticism and notion that man was not much different than an animal.[18] Such was the typical Southern reaction against secular humanists.

Theological Conservatism in the South

In reaction to the growing threat against Christianity stemming from higher education, the *Evangelical and Literary Magazine*, a Southern publication, encouraged parents to:

1) Express their own view on religion to their children;
2) Distribute Christian apologetic material in public;
3) Promote "intelligent men to promote their cause";
4) Support institutions that subscribed to orthodox Christianity; &
5) Pray for the integrity of the colleges.[19]

In fact, "All Southern institutions of any importance adopted" a Christian apologetics program employed by "teachers who were specially trained to present the truths of the Bible as opposed to the

---

[18] C. Dorough, *The Bible Belt Mystique*, (Philadelphia: Westminster Press, 1974), 118.

[19] *Ibid.*, 120.

skeptical concepts that were being passed around."[20] As a direct result of this movement, 25 to 50 percent of total reading content in primary and secondary education became religious in sentiment. Though we don't fully know the total extent to which this Christian apologetic movement touched higher education – simply because many of the institutions for higher learning in the early- to mid-1800s have since disappeared – we do know of at least six major colleges and universities that incorporated *Evidences of Christianity* into their curriculum from the period of 1798 to 1860, half of them adopting the program within ten years before the secession of South Carolina.[21]

The Northern reaction to Enlightenment thinking was much different than the Southern. Not only were radical heresies such as Transcendentalism and Unitarianism becoming widespread, but even what was considered orthodox Christianity quickly became compromised. Historian Eugene D. Genovese observed that:

> The political ramifications of southern Christian theology were enormous. For at the very moment that the northern churches were embracing theological liberalism and abandoning the Word for a Spirit increasingly reduced to personal subjectivity, the southern churches were holding the line for Christian orthodoxy.[22]

---

[20] *Ibid.*, 121-122.

[21] *Ibid.*, 120-122.

[22] B. Kuklick and D.G. Hart, *Religious Advocacy and American History* (W.B. Eerdmans Pub. Co., 1997), 92.

Historian Gregg Singer refers to this subtle departure in northern churches as the "New England Theology," describing it as "a mediating position holding to much of the Evangelical position while yielding at other points, particularly in regard to the doctrines of the atonement, divine sovereignty, and justification, in the direction of the Transcendentalist thought."[23]

Old School Presbyterianism, primarily represented in the South, split over this issue in 1837. Since 1801, when the Northern Presbyterians joined the Congregationalists (the breeding ground for "New England Theology") to do missionary work in the Ohio Valley, there had been ambivalence on the part of the denomination's conservatives. As time progressed and the New School Presbyterians challenged the doctrine of original sin and traditional ecclesiology,[24] the conservative Southern wing became more and more impatient, leading to eventual detachment.

THE NORTHERN SOCIAL CRUSADE

It is vital to understand that this schism came about as much as a result of doctrine as it did practice. New England author Chard Powers Smith stated, "The number of Yankee leaders in the Age of Reform probably runs into the thousands, great Puritans[25] whose Grace was in a Perception of Utopia potential in the selfless instincts

---

[23] Singer, *A Theological Interpretation of American History*, 65.

[24] Crowther, *Southern Evangelicals and the Coming of the Civil War* (Lewiston NY: E. Mellen Press, 2000), 77-78.

[25] The 19th century definition of "Puritan" did not carry the same positive connotation as it does today in Reformed circles.

of men and in the amelioration of their lot."[26] It was this class of "great Puritans" who took over Northern sections of evangelical denominations. To Southerners, these modern "reformers" stood more in the tradition of Robespierre than that of Calvin. Southern Presbyterian minister Benjamin M. Palmer told his congregation in 1860 that, "The demon which erected its throne upon the guillotine in the days of Robespierre and Marat, which abolished the Sabbath, and worshipped reason in the person of a harlot, yet survives to work other horrors, of which those of the French revolution are but the type."[27] Historian Edward Crowther sheds light on this sentiment by explaining:

> The rage of reform, from "socialism," to feminism, to abolitionism, like the scientific methods of "modernism," fashioned the forbidden fruits of the belief that humanity had grown beyond the need for revelation and, now, considered itself better equipped by its own reason to reshape the world that God had formed in the beginning. An infidel and naive conception of human nature had yielded an unfounded belief in the perfectibility of humankind, a concept that now threatened to make the United States into an unchristian republic.[28]

Most students of American history will be able to quickly call to mind the radical and varied movements to which both Palmer and

---

[26] C.P. Smith, *Yankees and God* (Hermitage House, 1954), 343.

[27] Frank Moore, *The Rebellion Record*, Vol. 2 (New York: G.P. Putnam, 1861), 5.

[28] Crowther, *Southern Evangelicals and the Coming of the Civil War*, 129.

Crowther refer. After the failed 1848 socialist revolutions in Europe, a myriad of northern newspapers were taken over by atheistic immigrants now banned from their own countries. In the same year, the Quaker-led "women's rights" movement commenced at a Wesleyan church in Seneca Falls, N.Y. Abolitionists like Transcendentalist William Lloyd Garrison circulated propaganda pieces like *The Liberator* from the 1830s through the 1860s.[29]

It is critical to keep in mind that these social movements flowed directly from belief systems. The truth in the old adage that "Universalists think God too good to damn them, while Unitarians think they are too good to be damned"[30] contains more than simply differences concerning the nature of God and man. Mixing the radical notions of the Transcendentalists, Unitarians, and Universalists, who all believed man was basically good, with the "New England [Arminian] Theology," while introducing thousands of newly arrived socialist revolutionaries from Europe – all groups sprinkled with a utopian ideal – created the perfect recipe for the Northern social reform movements. Even those who still maintained an orthodox Christianity "held to a postmillennial theology [finding it easy] to cooperate with the Transcendentalists in nearly all of the reform movements."[31] "Everywhere societies

---

[29] W.D. Kennedy and A. Benson, *Red Republicans and Lincoln's Marxists: Marxism in the Civil War* (iUniverse.com, 2007).

[30] "Bacon's American Christianity," *The Nation* (New York, November 4, 1897), 358.

[31] Singer, *A Theological Interpretation of American History*, 73.

sprang up to serve some humane cause."[32] James Brewer Stewart explains the phenomenon this way:

> Like their eighteenth-century predecessors, powerful evangelists such as Charles G. Finney and Lyman Beecher urged their audiences that man, though a sinner, should nonetheless strive for holiness and choose a new life of sanctification. Free will once again took precedence over original sin, which was again redefined as voluntary selfishness. As in the 1750s, God was pictured as insisting that the "saved" perform acts of benevolence, expand the boundaries of Christ's kingdom, and recognize a personal responsibility to improve society. Men and women again saw themselves playing dynamic roles in their own salvation and preparing society for the millennium. By the thousands they flocked to the Tract Society, the Sunday School Union, the temperance and peace organizations, and the Colonization Society.[33]

While it is not the focus of this work to study connections existing between European socialists, the Republican party, the "Women's Rights" movement, Abolitionism, and Finneyism, let it be noted that to characterize these connections as "overlapping" would be an understatement.

To the Southern mind only one thing truly mattered though. All of these societies and movements held to an ultimate authority

---

[32] E.S. Gaustad, *A Religious History of America* (Harper & Row, 1966), 179.

[33] J.B. Stewart, *Holy Warriors: The Abolitionists and American Slavery* (Hill and Wang, 1976), 35.

residing outside of Scripture. To illustrate this truth, let us briefly examine one of the more prominent movements originating directly before the War Between the States and continuing into the present time. Let us discover the true roots of the feminist movement.

Mathilde Anneke, both a German "Forty-eighter" and prominent American feminist, said, in reference to the "Women's Rights" campaign, "Reason, which we recognize as our highest and only law-giver, commands us to be free."[34] Elizabeth Cady Stanton, who later published the alternative *Women's Bible* in 1895, stated "The Bible and the Church have been the greatest stumbling blocks in the way of women's emancipation."[35] Susan B. Anthony was even more specific when she maintained that "out of the doctrine of original sin grew the crimes and miseries of asceticism, celibacy and witchcraft; women becoming the victim of all these delusions."[36]

To the casual observer, the "Women's Suffrage Movement," as it's often called, was all about the right to vote. This idea could not be further from the truth. The tenets of women's "emancipation" go much deeper than a mere right to vote. Their purpose was to overturn the social order by replacing biblical calling with individual desire. Rheta Childe Dorr proclaimed, "Woman's place is in the Home but Home is not contained within the four walls . . .

---

[34] "Odd Wisconsin Archives: Truly Radical Feminist," Wisconsin Historical Society, April 4, 2005.

[35] Barbara Walker, *Man Made God: A Collection of Essays* (Seattle: Stellar House Publishing, 2010), 267.

[36] M.D. Pellauer, *Toward a Tradition of Feminist Theology: The Religious Social Thought of Elizabeth Cady Stanton, Susan B. Anthony, and Anna Howard Shaw* (Carlson, 1991), 25.

Home is the community."[37] Dorr went on to describe a modern utopia rid of war and controlled by a maternal nature. A simple reading of the *Declaration of Sentiments* originating from the Seneca Falls Convention clearly shows what was happening. Whether right or wrong, policies like "no-fault" divorce, allowing female in the clergy and law professions, and the obliteration of societal distinctions between men and women were championed.[38]

The highly acclaimed Southern theologian Robert L. Dabney would later prophecy that "the only possible result of this movement will be, not the independence and equality of woman, but the substitution of the savage dependence of the slave-concubine, the 'weaker vessel' held and abused by brute force, for the benignant order of scriptural marriage."[39] The "women's rights" campaign was not heralded by the evangelical church as some modern interpretations would have us believe, unless what they mean by "evangelical" are Unitarians, Quakers, and liberal Wesleyans.

The purpose in this brief departure into the "women's rights" movement is to better understand its parallel movement: abolitionism. The suffragettes were active preceding the War Between the States, but it was not their influence that ultimately led to the war. In the antebellum period their influence was mainly relegated to the North and did not blossom fully until during and

---

[37] Rheta Childe Dorr, *What Eight Million Women Want* (Boston: Small, Maynard & Co., 1910), 327.

[38] Jeffrey Schultz, *Encyclopedia of Women in American Politics* (Phoenix: Oryx Press, 1999), 357-359.

[39] Dabney R.L., "Nature Cannot Revolutionize Nature," October 1, 1873.

after "Reconstruction." However, there is a connection between what happened in Seneca Falls in 1848 and what took place in South Carolina on December 20, 1860. Both abolitionism and women's liberation have been given charitable treatment in modern historical surveys, yet the impression left about each is generally incomplete. Just as the women's rights movement was not simply concerned with woman's suffrage, neither was abolitionism simply concerned with the right of slaves to be free. The Southerner's problem with radical abolitionism, as we shall see, had more to do with the rejection of biblical authority than it did the emancipation of slaves.

CHAPTER 2
SLAVERY IN THE CHRISTIAN SOUTH

IN JEFFERSON DAVIS'S post-war memoirs, *The Rise and Fall of the Confederate Government*, the former president submits, "To whatever extent the question of slavery may have served as an occasion, it was far from being the cause of the conflict."[40] Rev. Benjamin Palmer concurred by laying the conflict's cause at the feet of Northern atheism. "This spirit of atheism, which knows no God who tolerates evil, no Bible which sanctions law, and no conscience that can be bound by oaths and covenants, has selected us for its victims, and slavery for its issue."[41] There is no doubt that abolitionism played a huge part in driving both Southern secession and Northern aggression, especially in the theological realm. The politician and abolitionist Cassius Clay portrayed the entire institution of slavery as a "crime against man and God."[42] It was this type of extra-biblical dogmatism that eventually led to the fracturing of American Christianity along the Mason-Dixon line,

---

[40] Jefferson Davis, *The Rise and Fall Of the Confederate Government*, Vol. 1 (Kessinger Publishing, 2006), 78.

[41] Moore, *The Rebellion Record*, 5.

[42] Stanley Harrold, *The Abolitionists and the South, 1831-1861* (Lexington, Ky.: University Pess of Kentucky, 1999), 84.

and in turn – with its analogous political controversies – led to secession and war. In order to proceed in our understanding of the theological climate that ultimately caused this sectional friction, we must first understand a few things regarding the nature of the "peculiar" institution of slavery.

The Middle Passage

Unfortunately, there are a great many misunderstandings most modern Americans – including Southerners – tend to accept when it comes to the topic of early American slavery. Space does not exist here to address every misconception, but a few of them should be surveyed in order to develop a better understanding of the conflict. Knowing the political situation will help us understand the theological situation.

One of the first subjects that must be clarified is the nature of the "Middle Passage." Of the total number of African immigrants brought to the New World only 6 percent were brought to the United States,[43] most of them eventually winding up in the South (especially after the Northern states progressively found the institution to be impractical). This transition took place in what became known as the "Triangle Trade," in which Northeastern maritime towns – mainly in Connecticut and Rhode Island – would transport and trade southern tobacco and northern rum to different ports along the "Ivory Coast" of Africa. In return, slaves and gold dust would be taken to the Caribbean at which point they would be bartered for different forms of currency, sugar, and molasses (in

---

[43] W.D. Kennedy, *Myths of American Slavery* (Pelican Pub. Co., 2003), 44.

order to continue rum production).[44] Human beings were treated like animals. Close quarters, disease, hunger, thirst, beatings, and death all characterized the journey from the Ivory Coast to the New World.[45] Although "Only a few New England merchants actually engaged in the slave trade . . . all of them profited by it [and] lived off it."[46] The significance of this reality lies in an understanding of why Southerners tended to view Northerners as hypocrites. After the war, former Confederate soldier Robert Cave sarcastically remarked about a time when "even the pious sons of New England were slave owners and deterred by no conscientious scruples from plying the slave trade with proverbial Yankee enterprise."[47]

If we take a survey of one Northern maritime center, New York City, we can better understand the frustration that existed among vilified Southerners. In 1760 New York alone had more than 20,000 slaves in residence.[48] By 1822, slave-grown cotton had become 40 percent of New York's domestic exports (the North being the country's hub for cotton export).[49] "During peak years in 1859 and 1860, at least two slave ships left from New York every month, according to one cautious estimate. Most could hold between 600 and 1,000 slaves. So in each of those years,

---

[44] A. Farrow, J. Lang, and J. Frank, *Complicity: How the North Promoted, Prolonged, and Profited from Slavery* (Random House Publishing Group, 2006), 50.

[45] *Ibid.*, 106-108.

[46] *Ibid.*, 48.

[47] R.C. Cave, *The Men in Gray* (Confederate Veteran, 1911), 22.

[48] A. Farrow et al., *Complicity: How the North Promoted, Prolonged, and Profited from Slavery*, 214.

[49] *Ibid.*, 215.

New York ships might have carried as many as 20,000 new Africans into bondage."[50] By this time slave trading was technically illegal in the United States, but there were still rich markets in Cuba and Brazil. In 1863, the New York Draft rioters killed scores of blacks and set fire to a colored orphan asylum in reaction to Abraham Lincoln's *Emancipation Proclamation*.[51] How can such findings be consistent with the modern idea that the North was filled with charitable Christians who cared for nothing more than the plight of the Negro? The answer lies in the North's economic (and ultimately religious) reason for supporting the "free soil" movement.

RACISM AND THE PERPETUATION OF SLAVERY

Today, many Americans think that the South was (and perhaps still is) "racist central," while the North uniformly believed in the brotherhood of all men. Nothing could be further from the truth. Again, in the post-war memoirs of Jefferson Davis, the defeated president maintained that the Northern reason for fighting against the "extension of slavery" in the territories was less than sincere. Davis writes:

> [The idea of letting slaveholders into the territories] does not, never did, and never could, imply the addition of a single slave to the number already existing. The question was merely whether the slaveholder should be permitted to go, with his slaves, into territory (the common property of all) into which the non-slaveholder could go with his

---

[50] *Ibid.*, 122.
[51] *Ibid.*

property of any sort. There was no proposal nor desire on the part of the Southern States to reopen the slave-trade, which they had been foremost in suppressing, or to add to the number of slaves. It was a question of the distribution, or dispersion, of the slaves, rather than of the 'extension of slavery.'[52]

In short, what Davis is saying is that the North opposed the constitutional right for slave owners to transport their slaves into the territories for reasons other than a concern for slaves themselves.

There is little doubt that the North's disposition towards "Negroes" was hardly morally superior to the South's. In *Democracy in America*, foreign observer Alexis de Tocqueville discovered that "race prejudice seems stronger in those states that have abolished slavery than in those where it still exists, and nowhere is it more intolerant than in those states where slavery was never known."[53] Abraham Lincoln himself is often quoted as being "in favor of the [white] race" and having "no purpose to introduce political and social equality between the white and black races."[54] Lyman Trumbull, a Radical Republican senator from Illinois, summed up his state's sentiment by affirming, "Our people want nothing to do with the Negro."[55] Historian Mitchell Snay summarizes that "even the most

---

[52] Davis, *The Rise and Fall of the Confederate Government*, Vol. I, 7.

[53] A. Tocqueville, *Democracy in America* (HarperCollins Publishers, 2007), 182.

[54] A. Lincoln, *The Collected Works of Abraham Lincoln* (Wildside Press, 2008), 402.

[55] T.J. DiLorenzo, *The Real Lincoln: A New Look at Abraham Lincoln, His Agenda, and an Unnecessary War* (Three Rivers Press, 2003), 28.

committed abolitionists often had trouble perceiving blacks as 'beloved' brothers"[56] as the historical record indicates.[57] The state laws of the North certainly reflected this view, one example being *The Revised Code* of Indiana which declared that:

> All contracts with Negroes were null and void; any white person encouraging Negroes to enter the state was subjected to a $500 dollar fine; Negroes and mulattos were not allowed to vote; no Negro or mulatto having even one-eighth part of Negro blood could legally marry a white person – an act punishable by ten year's imprisonment and a fine of up to $5,000; any person counseling or encouraging interracial marriage was subject to a fine of up to $1,000; Negroes and mulattos were forbidden from testifying in court against white people, from sending their children to public schools, or from holding any political office.[58]

The obvious next question is, "If it was not for the plight of the slave, why did the North attempt to threaten an institution that had made it so prosperous?" There are many possible answers, but I know of no testimony more direct and authoritative than Lincoln's Secretary of State William Seward who explained that "the motive of those who protested against the extension of slavery had always

---

[56] J.R. McKivigan and M. Snay, *Religion and the Antebellum Debate Over Slavery* (University of Georgia Press, 1998), 148.

[57] S. Harrold, *The Abolitionists and the South, 1831-1861* (University Press of Kentucky, 1999), 98.

[58] *Ibid.*, 26.

really been concern for the welfare of the white man, and not an unnatural sympathy for the Negro."[59] Lincoln echoed this view himself in 1854 stating, "We want them [the territories] for the homes of free white people. This they cannot be, to any considerable extent, if slavery shall be planted within them."[60] Again in 1860, "their places [would] be, *pari passu*, filled up by free white laborers [after the completion of Lincoln's colonization plan]."[61] Author Lyle H. Lanier sums it up this way: "Because slave-holding was the acid test as to whether a state would remain agrarian or become eventually industrial, the Northern leaders wished that no more slave states should be carved from the Western territories."[62] In short, the typical Northerner was against the "extension of slavery" primarily in order to keep black labor from undercutting white labor and to dilute Southern congressional representation. In the words of Rev. James Henley Thornwell, "To exclude slaveholding is . . . to exclude the south."[63]

---

[59] *Ibid.*, 22.

[60] A. Lincoln, *The Collected Works of Abraham Lincoln*, (Wildside Press, 2008), 306.

[61] H. Holzer, *Lincoln at Cooper Union: The Speech That Made Abraham Lincoln President* (Simon & Schuster, 2006), 273.

[62] Twelve Southerners, *I'll Take My Stand: The South and the Agrarian Tradition* (Louisiana State University Press, 2006), 84.

[63] B.M. Palmer and J.H. Thornwell, *The Life and Letters of James Henley Thornwell* (Whittet & Shepperson, 1875), 602.

PLANTATION LIFE

If modern Americans were able to see the way most slaves lived during the antebellum period they would probably be surprised. British observer James S. Buckingham discovered:

> From all I could perceive or learn, the condition of the domestic servants, or slaves of the household, was quite as comfortable as that of servants in the middle ranks of life in England. They are generally well-fed, well-dressed, attentive, orderly, respectful, and easy to be governed, but more by kindness than by severity.[64]

This snapshot of slave life hardly resembles what modern Americans are typically led to believe through the education and entertainment industries. Masters that treated their slaves with respect are not supposed to exist – but they did.

According to antebellum whites, there were many planters who dealt with their slaves in a humane fashion. Walter Peterson, for example, recalled that in Alabama 'many slaveholders were kind masters.' Philip H. Jones of Louisiana asserted that 'Many owners were humane and kind and provided well for them [slaves].' According to Amanda Washington, among the planters '*Noblesse oblige* was recognized everywhere, and we felt bound to treat kindly the class dependent on us.' The

---

[64] J.S. Buckingham, *The Slave States of America* (Fisher, Son & Co., 1842), 131.

testimony of the white witnesses is borne out by those of the former slaves.[65]

In the *Slave Narratives* – the cumulative result of two years of in-depth interviews surveying over 2,000 former slaves by the Works Project Administration – former slaves were able to voice their own opinion on plantation life. Nobel prize winner Robert Fogel's and Stanley L. Engerman's work *Time on the Cross* makes a study of these narratives, demonstrating "that nowhere in the Western Hemisphere were slaves better treated and cared for than in the South."[66] The authors concluded that "60 to 80 percent of all respondents had only positive things to say about their masters and their life during slave days."[67] Another way to assess the slave's quality of life is to look at the rate of population increase. We can do this by comparing the number of live births with the number of deaths. In 1860, the Southern slave population was shown to have increased by 23 percent, while the Northern black population only increased 1.7 percent.[68] In the 1850 U.S. Census, which included a survey on the prevalence of certain disabilities, something even more startling emerges. One of every 1,000 white persons was deaf, dumb, blind, insane, or idiotic. In Northern states, 1 out of every 506 black persons had the same handicaps. For Southern slaves it was merely 1 in 1,464

---

[65] J.W. Blassingame, *The Slave Community: Plantation Life in the Antebellum South* (Oxford University Press, 1979), 71, 263-264.

[66] Kennedy, *Myths of American Slavery*, 91.

[67] *Ibid*.

[68] U.S. Bureau of the Census, "Population of the United States in 1860" (Government Printing Office, 1864).

persons who possessed them.⁶⁹ In addition, free blacks in the South shared about equivalent economic prosperity with their Southern white neighbors,⁷⁰ and while "it is true that in non-slaveholding States the blacks are free in theory . . . In practice their freedom often leads to misery and degradation, and not unfrequently to oppression from . . . white associate[s]."⁷¹ Rev. Dabney firmly opposed the charge by radical abolitionists such as Transcendentalist William Lloyd Garrison and Spiritualist Harriet Beecher Stowe in their attempt to paint Southern slavery as a brutal and evil arrangement in and of itself; an accusation almost universally believed to this day. Later Dabney would write in *A Defense of Virginia and the South*:

> Let it be understood . . . that we are not inquiring into the moral character of that thing which Abolitionists paint as domestic slavery; a[s] something horrid with the groans of oppressed innocence and the clang of unrighteous stripes; a[s] something which aims to reduce a man to a brute, and denies him his natural right to serve his Creator and save his soul. We begin by asserting that these things, if they

---

[69] U.S. Bureau of the Census, "The Seventh Census of the United States: 1850" (Robert Armstrong, Public Printer, 1853).

[70] Kennedy, *Myths of American Slavery*, 28.

[71] "Management of Slaves," *The American Farmer* (Baltimore: September 1846), 77.

ever exist in fact, are not domestic slavery, but the abuses of it.[72]

The Southern Christian consensus did not permit the severe abuses painted as "common" by Northern abolitionists. Even Frederick Douglass admitted that, "Public opinion is, indeed, an unfailing restraint upon the cruelty and barbarity of masters, overseers, and slave-drivers, whenever and wherever it can reach them."[73] Unfortunately, this public opinion was out of reach on Northeastern slave vessels. The shockingly different experience slaves underwent during the Middle Passage, as opposed to plantation life, can be summed up with these words: "For better or worse, the lord of the plantation had to coexist with his slaves. The slave trader had only to deliver them."[74] However, there was an even greater reason for this phenomenon, and it has to do with Southern Christianity.

COTTON FIELD MEETS MISSION FIELD

In the early part of the 19th century, the South maintained a Reformed understanding in the face of the growing threat of European rationalism. As a consequence, while a few Northerners were justifying their interactions with slavery by appealing to pre-

---

[72] R.L. Dabney, A Defence of Virginia: (and Through Her, of the South) in Recent and Pending Contests Against the Sectional Party (E.J. Hale, 1867), 98.

[73] F. Douglass, *My Bondage and My Freedom*, (Miller, Orton & Mulligan, 1855), 61.

[74] Farrow *et al*, *Complicity*, 108.

Darwinian naturalists, the South was stalwart in a "providential" view of the institution. Though Rev. Dabney perceived the slave trade as an "iniquitous traffick"[75] – as Exodus 21:16 affirms with its indictment of man-capture – he likewise held that "we [the people of Virginia] have no cause . . . to lament the condition which Providence had assigned us, in placing this African Race among us."[76] Dabney's reason was simple. God, in His sovereignty, had exposed a great many nonbelievers from foreign nations to the light of the Gospel, thereby bringing good out of evil. Dabney asked:

> . . . was it nothing that they [the slaves] should be brought, by the relation of servitude, under the consciences and Christian zeal of a Christian people, in circumstances which most powerfully enlisted their sense of responsibility, and gave free scope to their labour of love? Let the blessed results answer, of a nation of four millions lifted, in four generations, out of idolatrous debasement, "sitting clothed, and in their right mind;" of more than half a million adult communicants in Christian churches! . . . This much-abused system has thus accomplished for the Africans, amidst universal opposition and obloquy, more than all the rest of the Christian world together has accomplished for the rest of the heathen.[77]

Historian John W. Blassingame explains Dabney's sentiment this way: "One of the legacies Southern churches inherited from the

---

[75] R.L. Dabney, *A Defence of Virginia*, 27.
[76] *Ibid.*, 303.
[77] *Ibid.*, 281.

Reformation was the duty to proselytize heathens."[78] Many Southern denominations, at the petition of their congregants, launched slave mission efforts toward the middle part of the 19th century in which a traveling preacher would care for the needs of individual slaves on their plantations.[79] In an 1863 address by ninety-six ministers in the Confederacy, entitled, *An Address to Christians Throughout the World*, this evangelistic mission was fully and clearly defined:

> Most of us have grown up from childhood among the slaves; all of us have preached to and taught them the word of life; have administered to them the ordinances of the Christian church; sincerely love them as souls for whom Christ died; we go among them freely and know them in health and sickness, in labor and rest, from infancy to old age. We are familiar with their physical and moral condition, and alive to all their interests; and we testify in the sight of God, that the relation of master and slave among us, however we may deplore abuses in this, as in other relations of mankind, is not incompatible with our holy Christianity, and that the presence of the Africans in our land is an occasion of gratitude on their behalf, before God; seeing that thereby Divine Providence has brought them where missionaries of the cross may freely proclaim to them the word of salvation, and the work is not interrupted by agitating fanaticism. The South has done

---

[78] Blassingame, *The Slave Community*, 71.
[79] *Ibid.*, 94-95.

more than any people on earth for the christianization of the African race. The condition of slaves here is not wretched, as northern fictions would have men believe, but prosperous and happy.[80]

Although many northern abolitionists believed the gospel was not being delivered to the slaves through their masters – otherwise in their minds, the slaves would be set free – the historical account demonstrates the exact opposite. When a committee of South Carolina's Episcopal Church asked ministers what they taught slaves in 1843,[81] it learned that:

> In preaching, the same great subjects seem to have been inculcated, which are insisted on in white congregations, viz. our fall in Adam, and our redemption in Christ – the sinfulness and lost state of man, and the glorious privileges to which the Gospel admits him; the necessity of repentance, faith, and holy obedience. To these subjects are added, as occasion may allow, the peculiar duties arising out of the condition of servants in relation to their owners, fellow-servants and families.[82]

John W. Blassingame likewise affirms,

---

[80] Conference of Ministers, Assembled at Richmond, Va., *An Address to Christians Throughout the World* (Parrish & Willingham, 1863), 7.

[81] Blassingame, *The Slave Community*, 88.

[82] Diocese of South Carolina Council, *Journal of the Proceedings of the Fifty-Fourth Annual Convention of the Protestant Episcopal Church, in South Carolina* (The Diocese, 1843), 38.

> White ministers emphasized oral instruction, memorization, interrogatories, and singing in their efforts to christianize the slaves. Slaves memorized the Lord's Prayer, the Ten Commandments, and many aspects of the denomination's liturgy. Ministers, bishops, and masters often questioned the slaves to make sure they understood what had been taught, . . . [and] when it came time to join a church, slaves exercised their own choice, demonstrating their autonomy. Slaves catechized by Episcopalians or Roman Catholics persisted in joining Baptists and Methodists."[83]

Such testimonies may sound unusual to modern ears. "Masters would share the gospel with their slaves and allow them to choose their own church? Surely if they partook in such actions it must have been for greater control! Perhaps in addition to the gospel, obedience to their masters was heavily emphasized?" Such a question can be answered by examining the *Slave Narrative's* suggestion that "only 15 percent of the Georgia slaves who had heard antebellum whites preach recalled admonitions to obedience."[84] This despite all the fear stirred up by abolitionist rhetoric designed specifically to instigate slave insurrections. Lest one think that "15 percent" is still too high a percentage, let us not forget all the sermons aimed at the way masters were to treat their slaves.

---

[83] Blassingame, *The Slave Community*, 89-90.
[84] *Ibid.*, 89.

Not only were verses such as *Colossians* 3:22, *Ephesians* 6:5, and *1 Peter* 2:18 delivered by preachers to encourage slaves to "obey [their] earthly masters," but so were *Ephesians* 6:9 and *Colossians* 4:1, which prodded masters to "give up threatening" and "grant to your slaves justice and fairness." Southern Episcopal bishop George W. Freeman said, "It is the duty of masters not only to be merciful to their servants, but to do everything in their power to make their situation comfortable, and to put forth all reasonable effort to render them contented and happy."[85] This principle did not fade in the midst of tough economic difficulty, either. In 1851, a Methodist paper, after cotton prices had dropped, told masters not to overwork their slaves.[86] In an 1851 Southern Baptist publication titled *The Duties of Christian Masters*, Rev. A.T. Holmes exclaims, "Equity pleads the right of humanity . . . and, in the conscientious discharge of duty, prompts the master to such treatment of his servant as would be desired on his part, were their positions reversed."[87]

His reasoning? "The exercise of right and authority on the part of the master, with reference only to his interest, uninfluenced by kindness to his servant, must incur the displeasure of Him with whom there is no respect of persons."[88] Although it is logical that a "planter ordinarily could not afford to starve, torture, or work . . . [his slaves] to death,"[89] it was an understanding and belief in God's

---

[85] *Ibid.*, 269.

[86] Crowther, *Southern Evangelicals and the Coming of the Civil War*, 100.

[87] H.N. McTyeire *et al.*, *Duties of Masters to Servants: Three Premium Essays* (Southern Baptist Publication Society, 1851), 133.

[88] *Ibid.*, 133.

[89] Blassingame, *The Slave Community*, 271.

sovereignty that motivated Southern Christians to act in a charitable manner. Holland N. McTyeire, a Methodist bishop from New Orleans, confirms this idea when he warns, "As you treat your servants on earth, so will your Master in heaven treat you."[90] The effects of this missions effort can be seen in the September 1845 edition of *American Farmer*, in an article titled "Management of Slaves," by the Barbour County (Ala.) Agriculture Society, which reported that:

> Our laws require us to attend to the happiness of our slaves; and our missionary establishment, with its ample support by us, shows that we acknowledge the obligation on us, to promote the well-being of our slaves. But even more – actual statistical returns show that religion is more prevalent among the slaves of the South than the free blacks of the Northern States, and universal opinion concurs in giving them a higher moral character.[91]

THE SLAVE AS HUMAN

In addition to desiring to please God, Southern slaveholders also recognized something just as fundamental from the Scriptures: An African slave was still a human being. It is neither something new nor a coincidence that modern "creation science" flourishes in the Bible-belt and not in the North where, starting in the 1830s, pre-

---

[90] H.N. McTyeire and T.O. Summers, *Duties of Christian Masters* (Southern Methodist Publishing House, 1859), 125-126.

[91] "Management of Slaves," *The American Farmer* (Baltimore: September 1846), 77.

Darwinian scientist Samuel George Morton, one of Philadelphia's most eminent physicians, "... used measurements from his world-famous collection of skulls to show that black people had the smallest cranial capacity of all human types and were doomed to inferiority."[92] In *Crania Americana*, Morton "presumed that the Bible had been misread. Caucasians and Negroes were too different to both be descended from Adam through Noah. Morton speculated that God must have intervened at the time of the Flood to reshape mankind."[93] It is no wonder that the Philadelphian's most ardent critic, John Bachman, was a minister from Charleston.

Morton disciples Josiah Nott and Louis Agassiz published a 700-page treatise entitled *Types of Mankind* in 1854 which "proved" that blacks were a separate species than whites. Presbyterian Thomas Smyth, another Charleston minister, countered with *Unity of the Human Race* which *The Watchman and Observer* of Richmond, *Southern Baptist* and *Southern Baptist Advocate* carried, enabling the work to become widely approved.[94] In Josiah Nott's paper *The Mulatto a Hybrid*, "Nott declared that science – not the Bible – must decide the true origins of mankind . . . [proposing] that God must have made separate races of men, just as He had made separate species of animals."[95] Though there were many men in the North who did not accept this interpretation, the headquarters of opposition lay in the South. Prominent Southern theologian James

---

[92] Farrow, *et al.*, *Complicity*, 182.

[93] Ibid., 186.

[94] Crowther, *Southern Evangelicalism and the Coming of the Civil War*, 97-98.

[95] Ibid., 187.

SACRED CONVICTION

Henley Thornwell – an opponent of higher biblical criticism as previously mentioned – in a sermon entitled *The Rights and Duties of Masters*, had this to say about the "race" scientists' thesis:

> The Negro is of one blood with ourselves – that he has sinned as we have, and that he has an equal interest with us in the great redemption. Science, falsely so called, may attempt to exclude him from the brotherhood of humanity ... but the instinctive impulses of our nature combined with the plainest declarations of the word of God, lead us to recognize in his form and lineaments – his moral, religious and intellectual nature – the same humanity in which we glory as the image of God. We are not ashamed to call him our brother.[96]

And "brother" he became to most of families who not only gained from his labor, but frequently freed him and allowed him to attain their level of success. In W.J. Cash's highly acclaimed book *The Mind of the South*, the author describes plantation culture as a

> ... society in which the infant son of the planter was commonly suckled by a black mammy, in which gray old black men were his most loved story-tellers, in which black stalwarts were among the chiefest heroes and mentors of his boyhood, and in which his usual, often practically his only, companions until he was past the age of puberty were the black boys (and girls) of the plantation.[97]

---

[96] J.H. Thornwell, *The Rights and Duties of Masters* (Walker & James, 1850), 11.

[97] W.J. Cash, *The Mind of the South* (Vintage Books, 1991), 49.

To this day the impact slaves have had on Southern whites and vice versa is observable. "Southern whites not only adapted their language and religion to that of the slaves but also adapted agricultural practices, sexual attitudes, rhythm of life, architecture, food and social relations to African patterns."[98] In fact, the relationship between blacks and whites was so intimate that in the 1847 Charleston based *Southern Presbyterian Review*, it was reported that, "Our children catch the very dialect of our servants, and lisp all their perversions of the English tongue, long before they learn to speak it correctly."[99] In turn, the reforming effects of the church turned the slaves from polygamy to monogamy[100] and from animistic religions to Christianity. For Northern abolitionists though, this simply was not enough.

---

[98] Blassingame, *The Slave Community*, 101.

[99] An Association of Ministers in the Town of Columbia, S.C., *Southern Presbyterian Review* I, (June 1847), 90.

[100] *Ibid.*, 161-163.

CHAPTER 3
A Higher Law

THE NORTH'S MOTIVATION in opposing Southern culture, as we have already seen, was greatly connected with "white" economic interest. However, this was merely the tip of an iceberg, carrying religious differences. Historian and member of the "Southern Agrarians" Frank Lawrence Owsley highlighted one of the major differences between both regions when he wrote,

> "The one [North] was extreme centralization, the other [South] was extreme decentralization; the one was nationalistic and the other provincial; the first was called Federalism, the other State Rights, but in truth the first should have been called Unitarianism and the second Federalism."[101]

Owsley rightly recognized the fact that religious beliefs in the North determined political motives, not the other way around. Though "the civilization of the North was coarse and materialistic . . . [and the] South was scant of shows, but highly refined and sentimental,"[102] there existed deeper forces at work than economic needs and cultural rhythm. Unitarianism, and other Yankee

---

[101] Twelve Southerners, *I'll Take My Stand*, 85.

[102] E.A. Pollard, *The Lost Cause: A New Southern History of the War of the Confederates.* (E. B. Treat & Co., 1866), 180.

religious movements previously mentioned, with their emphasis on man's perfectibility and the hope of utopia demanded a centralized government in order to enact "reforms" and pay for infrastructure projects[103] – two objectives that both Southerners as a whole[104] and the Christian majority in the South[105] thoroughly disagreed with. They believed instead that "the structures in society mattered far less than the moral caliber of those operating within society."[106] Creating such a government demanded the erosion of "state's rights," enshrined in the Constitution, and supplying such a government with resources demanded a large revenue base. For many unorthodox Northerners, such as Transcendentalist Ralph Waldo Emerson, "socialism [had] . . . done good service."[107] Unfortunately for Dixie, "the material prosperity of the North was greatly dependent on the Federal Government,"[108] and the federal government in turn was greatly dependent on a protectionist tariff which targeted and victimized the South.

---

[103] DiLorenzo, *The Real Lincoln*, 2.

[104] Twelve Southerners, *I'll Take My Stand*, 76.

[105] Crowther, *Southern Evangelicals and the Coming of the Civil War*, 9.

[106] *Ibid.*, 35.

[107] E.W. Emerson, ed., *The Complete Works of Ralph Waldo Emerson: The Conduct of Life* (Houghton, Mifflin, 1859), 97.

[108] United States War Dept., *The War of the Rebellion: A Compilation of the Official Records of the Union and Confederate Armies*, (Govt. Print. Off., 1900), 82.

Northern Religion and the Protectionist Tariff

In 1816, the Tariff was first introduced as a way to "repay" New England's manufacturing industry for the hit it took during the War of 1812. International imports were taxed to keep Southerners buying goods produced in Northern factories (unfortunately in turn making it harder for Europe to purchase Southern cotton). Soon however, the Tariff meant much more to the North than mere compensation; it produced the lifeblood of the federal bureaucracy. The 1828 "Tariff of Abominations," charged by John C. Calhoun to be "unconstitutional,"[109] raised the rate to 41 percent.[110] Before a compromise could be reached, South Carolina threatened to nullify the federal law, instigating a constitutional battle that foreshadowed the War for Southern Independence more than thirty years later.

It is worth noting that "many of those who would soon be the leaders of Old School Presbyterianism in the South after the division of 1837 refused to support South Carolina and Calhoun because many of the leaders of this movement were very liberal in their theological outlook."[111] (Though Rev. Dabney did in a passing comment refer to the Tariff as "unjust."[112]) This sentiment of course changed as radical abolitionists who subverted Scripture gained influence in the North.

---

[109] DiLorenzo, *The Real Lincoln*, 63.

[110] G.E. Croscup and E.D. Lewis, *History Made Visible: A Synchronic Chart and Statistical Tables of United States History* (Windsor Pub. Co., 1910), 62.

[111] Singer, *A Theological Interpretation of American History*, 83.

[112] Dabney, *A Defence of Virginia*, 43.

Economist Thomas DiLorenzo believes that by the eve of secession, "the primary source of federal revenue was tariff revenue."[113] With the Tariff being the "centerpiece of the Republican program"[114] and the first Republican president, Abraham Lincoln, supporting the "Morill Tariff bill, which proposed raising the tariff rate by as much as 250 percent on some items,"[115] South Carolina had had enough.

Former U.S. ambassador James Williams wrote in 1862, "It would appear to be an error to suppose that the manufacturers [Northeasterners], as a class, are in reality endeavouring to achieve the destruction of the institution of slavery. They only seek, through a protective tariff, to divide with the planters the earnings of slave labour."[116] While a significant portion of the North did not really care one way or the other whether the South kept slaves or not, they did find it convenient "to borrow the language of the abolitionists and [clothe] the struggle in a moral garb"[117] when necessary. Confederate journalist Edward A. Pollard exclaimed:

> The North naturally found or imagined in slavery the leading cause of the distinctive civilization of the South, its higher sentimentalism, and its superior refinements of

---

[113] Dilorenzo, *The Real Lincoln*, 63.

[114] R.F. Bensel, *Yankee Leviathan: The Origins of Central State Authority in America, 1859-1877* (Cambridge University Press, 1990), 73.

[115] Dilorenzo, *The Real Lincoln*, 63.

[116] J.B. Williams and J.B. Hopkins, *The South Vindicated* (Longman, Green, 1862). 59-60.

[117] Singer, *A Theological Interpretation of American History*, 84.

scholarship and manners. It revenged itself on the cause, diverted its envy in an attack upon slavery, and defamed the institution as the relic of barbarism and the sum of all villainies.[118]

This idea that "slavery was a sin" seemed to justify the plundering of the South whose residents, after all, needed to be made better citizens due to the stain of the corrupting institution of slavery. Educator Francis Wayland expresses this sentiment in an 1865 letter to President Lincoln in which he exclaims, "It has been a war of education and patriotism against ignorance and barbarism."[119]

In short, the North needed the South in order to finance its ideal world. In addition, the belief in human autonomy threatened social institutions that included a hierarchal structure such as patriarchy and slavery. Historian Edward R. Crowther comments,

> As the structural force of modernization and the intellectual force of transcendentalism created threats to southern society, their specific offspring, abolitionism and industrialization, brought intellectual challenges to the southern political and moral economies. Preachers, especially, found the romantic notions of human perfectibility a threat to their theological order. In their

---

[118] Pollard, *The Lost Cause*, 48.
[119] H. Barnard, *The American Journal of Education*, (1865), 815.

construction of things, patriarchy represented God's way of arranging a society stained by sin.[120]

It is lamentable that most historians simply do not connect the dots between religion, government, and economics when it comes to the war, leaving most to either insist that it was only about "state's rights" or, more often the case, that it was only about slavery. Indeed, both topics served as the palettes on which the struggle was painted, but neither answer truly addresses the religious assumptions at the base of the struggle. Southern clergyman understood this. This is why Methodist preacher J.W. Tucker could tell his Southern audience that, "your cause is the cause of God, the cause of Christ, of humanity. It is a conflict of truth with error – of Bible with Northern infidelity – of pure Christianity with Northern fanaticism."[121] In order to understand this fanaticism we must turn our attention to the religious nature of the slavery debate.

SLAVERY DEBATED

In 1845, a debate was held in Cincinnati, Ohio, between two local Presbyterian ministers. The topic of the debate was whether "slave-holding [was] in itself sinful, and the relationship between master and slave, a sinful relation?"[122] For many Northern Presbyterians the question had already been answered. The minister from Indiana, Rev. James Duncan, stated quite concretely in his 1840

---

[120] Crowther, *Southern Evangelicals and the Coming of the Civil War*, 52.

[121] O.V. Burton, *The Age of Lincoln* (Farrar, Straus and Giroux, 2008).

[122] J. Blanchard and N.L Rice, *A Debate on Slavery* (W.H. Moore & Co., 1846).

publication *A Treatise on Slavery* that, "In the whole volume of Divine providence, there is no one thing which shows the absolute necessity of a hell, more than the practice of involuntary, unmerited, hereditary slavery."[123] Clearly the impact of abolitionism was no longer contained in Transcendentalist, Unitarian, and Quaker communities. It had now infiltrated mainline denominations and "providence" was being redefined to coincide with this infiltration. A sizable minority of Northern Congregationalist and New School Presbyterians had, by the time of the Cincinnati debate, made the decision to "make slave holding a bar to christian fellowship, on the ground, that it is a heinous and scandalous sin."[124] It was in this context that abolitionist Rev. J. Blanchard and "traditional emancipationist"[125] Dr. N.L. Rice publically jousted. Author Walter D. Kennedy summarizes Blanchard's performance by saying, "in more than twenty-four hours of debate, the Radical Abolitionists' view could not be maintained . . . Rev. Blanchard used all his time in opening the Debate and yet did not once address the theme of the debate,"[126] instead focusing on the purported abuses within the chattel system. The closest thing resembling a moral argument

---

[123] J. Duncan, *A Treatise on Slavery* (American Anti-Slavery Society, 1840), 119.

[124] Blanchard and Rice, *A Debate on Slavery*, 194.

[125] I am calling those who believed in the progressive abolition of slavery "traditional emancipationists" and those who believed in the immediate emancipation of slavery "abolitionists." The latter term also incorporates the belief that slaveholders ought to be punished for their involvement in the "sinful" practice.

[126] W.D. Kennedy, *Myths of American Slavery*, 71-72.

maintaining the idea that the reality of slavery was in and of itself sinful came when Blanchard said:

> Abolitionists take their stand upon the New Testament doctrine of the natural equity of man, the one-bloodism of human kind; and upon those great principles of human rights, drawn from the New Testament, and announced in the American Declaration of Independence, declaring that all men have natural and inalienable rights to person, property and the pursuit of happiness.[127]

Notice that the appeal Blanchard made avoids directly addressing the actual issue. It also implies a "general" morality flowing from the principles of the New Testament and the Declaration of Independence rather than a clear statement based upon specific passages in Scripture. Rice picked up on this and decidedly focused on the issue of the debate – the issue that ended up splitting America's denominations – "Is slave-holding in and of itself sinful?" Rice's views regarding the perpetuation of the institution were one and the same with the overriding opinion of the South. He states, "In denying that slave-holding is in itself sinful, I do not defend slavery as an institution that ought to be perpetrated . . . I desire to see every slave free; not nominally free, as are the colored people in Ohio."[128]

---

[127] A. Himes, *The Sword of the Lord: The Roots of Fundamentalism in an American Family* (CreateSpace, 2010), 54.

[128] Blanchard and Rice, *A Debate on Slavery*, 33-34.

It is worth noting that "as of 1827 there were more than four times as many anti-slavery societies in the South as in the North."[129] However, the rise of abolitionism in the North, with the view that slaveholders should be punished and emancipation should happen immediately without compensation or any integration into Northern society, rendered the situation inverse by the time of the war. This did not mean that Southerners – even the less than 5% of whites who owned slaves[130] – were not ultimately opposed to the institution being perpetuated indefinitely. Robert E. Lee himself stated after the war that the extinction of slavery had "been long sought, though in a different way, and by none has it been more earnestly desired than by citizens of Virginia."[131]

Southerners, and other religious conservatives, were not blind to the abuses inherent in the slave system. Though life in America may possibly have been substantially better than life in Africa in many cases, this still did not negate the horrors of the Middle Passage or justify – however uncommon – the physical and emotional abuse slaves underwent. In fact, "there is overwhelmingly convincing evidence that a substantial number of Southern slaveholders never rested easy with their black species of

---

[129] T.E. Woods, *The Politically Incorrect Guide to American History* (Regnery Pub., 2004), 42.

[130] J.H. Franklin and A.A. Moss, *From Slavery to Freedom: A History of African Americans* (Knopf, 1994), 139. [". . . one family out of three owned slaves," though about half of these families owned under 10 slaves each. (J. Williams and J. B Hopkins, *The South Vindicated*), xxxii.]

[131] H.A. White, *Robert E. Lee and the Southern Confederacy, 1807-1870* (G.P. Putnam's Sons, 1897), 447.

property."[132] In the late 1850s Southerners wanted the slave trade stopped because of its association with man-capture which the Apostle Paul had castigated in *1 Timothy* 1:9-10. They reasoned that "The mild, humane system of slavery in the Southern states with the atrocities of the slave trade, . . . [brought] on the one the odium that attaches to the other."[133] This is why inherent in the Confederate Constitution is a ban on the slave trade and an allowance for each individual state to ban the chattel system in its own time and way.[134] "The perception that the evils of slavery could be diminished by the civilizing influence of Christianity was to be the hallmark of the South's opinion about the institution."[135]

The ethical component to this is just as important a consideration as the historical component. To illustrate, a slightly similar modern situation may be the consumer who abhors the reality of sweatshops yet cannot yet afford to purchase high end clothing. Such a person may not be comfortable with the situation, but they would perhaps rightfully defend themselves against the charge that they are evil for wearing affordable clothing. Another similar analogy might be a Christian welfare worker who believes that the government-based system they are employed in should not exist since charity is not to be compulsory, and the state is not mandated by God to provide charity. In addition, on the basis of 2

---

[132] Blassingame, *The Slave Community*, 79.

[133] Crowther, *Southern Evangelicals and the Coming of the Civil War*, 106.

[134] Constitution of the Confederate States of America, section 9, " the importation of negroes." Avalon Project.

[135] James Ronald Kennedy and W.D. Kennedy, *Was Jefferson Davis Right?* (Pelican Pub. Co., 1998), 15.

Thess. 3:10 and 1 Tim. 5:3-8, perhaps they notice sinful abuses within the system, abuses that are causing generational dependence and immoral or unhealthy lifestyles. They are not comfortable with the situation and therefore vote and work to progressively reform it. Yet, they do not quit their job since it is not sinful for them to have it, and the consequences of letting it go could make the situation even worse for those to whom they were seeking to minister to within it. Neither do they support an immediate abolition of the system since the cure may be worse than the disease. They would never defend the welfare system, but they would defend the idea that what they were doing was not in and of itself morally wrong according to a biblical standard. Such examples are not completely analogous in every way to the situation many slave-holders found themselves in, but they do present the same kind of moral dilemma.

Far from defending the institution of slavery as it was, Rice's goal was to defend against the unbiblical and arbitrary assertions of his opponent who "had attempted to appeal to the sympathies of the audience rather than making Biblical arguments to support the Radical Abolitionists theory that slavery in itself is sinful."[136] Rice charged, "I do not remember that the gentleman provided one argument to prove slave-holding in itself sinful unless he intended his appeal to the Constitutions of Ohio, Indiana, and Illinois to be so considered . . . [Yet] they are not the rule of our faith or of our morals."[137]

---

[136] W.D. Kennedy, *Myths of American Slavery*, 71-72. 78.
[137] Blanchard and Rice, *A Debate on Slavery*, 36.

Dr. Rice then proceeded to show the arbitrary nature of Blanchard's position by surveying biblical passages concluding that a form of the system was in fact endorsed by God and to call something sinful which God Himself had not called sinful was an affront to His moral nature. "And can we believe that if slaveholding were in itself sinful, God could have entered into a covenant with Abraham, requiring him not to liberate his slaves, but to circumcise them?"[138] Rice interrogated: "Even the law of Moses," he affirmed, "permitted the master to enforce obedience by chastisement [a characteristic not common to mere servants]."[139] When "A centurion came to Jesus in Capernaum, told him that his servant, (*douos*, slave) . . . was very ill, and besought him to heal him. What was the Saviour's reply? Did he denounce him as a man-stealer, a robber?"[140] Likewise, "Paul and Peter teach us, as plainly as language can teach, that there were in many of the churches, as at Ephesus and Colosse, both masters and slaves; and they give such directions to both, as cannot apply to employers and hired servants."[141] Although it can be seen that such statements were biblical in character, throughout the decades preceding the war these same arguments were presented over and over as abolitionists and their more conservative rivals debated the issue.

---

[138] *Ibid.*, 262.
[139] *Ibid.*, 131.
[140] *Ibid.*, 389.
[141] *Ibid.*, 473.

Hath God Said?

Abolitionists who tried to get beyond the Bible, or reinterpret it to match their agenda, became the real reason that drove orthodox Christians in the South to react in strong ways. It was truly a disagreement over ultimate authorities. Who decided what constituted a sin? God or man? The abolitionist perspective, not being rooted in Scripture, was therefore viewed as the philosophy of "atheism." Lyle H. Lanier sums up this period of history in his contribution to the famous work *I'll Take My Stand*. He writes,

> The South threw up a defense mechanism [against abolitionist attacks]. The ministers searched the Scriptures by day and night and found written, language which could not be misunderstood, a biblical sanction of slavery . . . Partly as a result of this searching of the Scriptures there took place a religious revival . . . The South became devoutly orthodox and literal in its theology. But the abolitionists were not willing to accept scriptural justification of slavery. There was an attempt to prove the wrongfulness of slavery by the same sacred book, but, finding this impossible, many abolitionists repudiated the Scriptures as of divine origin. Partly as a result, the North lost confidence in orthodoxy and tended to become deistic.[142]

"Deistic" as they were at the root, the abolitionists forged ahead with their assertions that slavery was morally evil. According to historian Mark Noll:

> Foremost in this group [of abolitionists] was William Lloyd Garrison, who in 1845 paid homage in *The Liberator* to

---

[142] Twelve Southerners, *I'll Take My Stand*, 81.

> Thomas Paine for providing him with intellectual resources for getting beyond the Bible . . . So inclined, Garrison no longer had any difficulty with biblical passages that seemed to countenance the legitimacy of slavery . . . Garrison's move was audacious and courageous, but his willingness to jettison the Bible if the Bible was construed as legitimating slavery was too radical for most of his fellow Americans.[143]

Harriet Beecher Stowe also had the same problem being "intimated [with] the cynical conclusion, which would become more common among secularists after the Civil War, that the Bible was easily manipulated to prove anything with regard to a problem like slavery that readers might desire."[144] Therefore, "the significance of Stowe's *Uncle Tom's Cabin* for the biblical debate over slavery lay in the novel's emotive power,"[145] not in its scriptural exegesis. While many Northerners bought into Stowe's arguments, (to the point in which Lincoln referred to her as "the little lady who started the big war") Southerners were not willing to for the simple reason that they "rejected romantic notions and human feelings as the source of religious knowledge."[146]

Stowe's brother Unitarian Rev. Henry Ward Beecher "conceded, a defense of slavery could be teased out of obscure,

---

[143] Noll, *The Civil War as a Theological Crisis*, 31-32.
[144] Ibid., 42.
[145] Ibid., 43-44.
[146] Crowther, *Southern Evangelicals and the Coming of the Civil War*, 16.

individual texts of Scripture, but surely the defining message of the Bible was something else entirely."[147]

There were likewise many abolitionists who didn't want to completely throw out the Bible or the Constitution – a document Garrison maintained was "a pact with the Devil."[148] They attempted instead to interpret both documents according to their own taste — eisegesis instead of exegesis. Some of the more sophisticated abolitionists such as New York Congregationalist George Cheever, who published *God Against Slavery,* "labored diligently . . . to show that Old Testament 'bondmen' and New Testament 'servants' were not slaves at all,"[149] a charge unfounded upon a closer examination of biblical languages, as Nathan L. Rice, using exegetical interpretation and citing "all commentators, critics, and theologians of any note,"[150] made abundantly clear in his debate with Jonathan Blanchard.[151] In 1861, Henry Van Dyke, the pastor of Brooklyn Presbyterian, expressed in a sermon entitled *The Character and Influence of Abolitionism* that:

> Abolitionism leads, in multitudes of cases, and by a logical process, to utter infidelity . . . One of its avowed principles is, that it does not try slavery by the Bible; but . . . it tries the Bible by the principles of freedom . . . This assumption,

---

[147] Noll, *The Civil War as a Theological Crisis,* 44-45.

[148] B. Schecter, *The Devil's Own Work: The Civil War Draft Riots and the Fight to Reconstruct America* (Walker & Company, 2007), 38.

[149] Noll, *The Civil War as a Theological Crisis,* 31-32.

[150] Blanchard and Rice, *A Debate on Slavery,* 319.

[151] *Ibid.,* 319, 383-388.

that men are capable of judging beforehand what is to be expected in a Divine revelation, is the cockatrice's egg, from which, in all ages, heresies have been hatched.[152]

Rev. Van Dyke was responding to assertions such as the one made by Presbyterian abolitionist Albert Barnes who wrote in *The Church and Slavery*,

> There are great principles in our nature, as God has made us, which can never be set aside by any authority of a professed revelation. If a book claiming to be a revelation from God, by any fair interpretation defended slavery, or placed it on the same basis as the relation of husband and wife, parent and child, guardian and ward, such a book would not and could not be received by the mass of mankind as a Divine revelation.[153]

It should come as no surprise that not only was Barnes tried by the church for his unorthodox views on original sin and the atonement, but he also introduced "higher criticism" to the public through his biblical commentaries. Van Dyke's reaction to Barnes was potent. He pointed out: "When the Abolitionist tells me that slaveholding is sin, in the simplicity of my faith in the Holy Scriptures, I point him to this sacred record, and tell him, in all candor, as my text does, that his teaching blasphemes the name of God and His doctrine."[154]

---

[152] H.J. Van Dyke, *The Character and Influence of Abolitionism* (H. Taylor, 1860), 29.

[153] A. Barnes, *The Church and Slavery* (Negro Universities Press, 1857), 193.

[154] Van Dyke, *The Character and Influence of Abolitionism*, 7.

Leonard Bacon, a Congregationalist from Connecticut, hit the nail on the head in 1846 when he stated, "The evidence that there were both slaves and masters of slaves in the churches founded and directed by the apostles, cannot be got rid of without resorting to methods of interpretation which will get rid of everything."[155] Essentially, he was accusing abolitionists of being irrational. Thornton W. Stringfellow, a Virginia Baptist preacher, pointed out the unchristian nature of such argumentation when he challenged,

> If slavery be thus sinful it behooves all Christians who are involved in the sin, to repent in dust and ashes . . . Sin in the sight of God is something which God in his Word makes known to be wrong, either by perceptive prohibition, by principles of moral fitness, or examples of inspired men, contained in the sacred volume. When these furnish no law to condemn human conduct, there is no transgression. Christians should produce a "thus saith the Lord" both for what they condemn as sinful, and for what they approve as lawful, in the sight of heaven.[156]

Edward Crowther summarizes the Southern position with the words:

> Having concluded that a literal reading of the infallible scripture sanctioned slavery, they determined that no other interpretation of the Bible existed. When some abolitionists

---

[155] L. Bacon, *Slavery Discussed in Occasional Essays, From 1833 to 1846* (Baker and Scribner, 1846), 180.

[156] D.G. Faust, *The Ideology of Slavery: Proslavery Thought in the Antebellum South, 1830-1860* (Louisiana State University Press, 1981), 138.

countered that the spirit behind the biblical passages called for an ethic counter to slavery, southerners questioned the way in which abolitionists read scripture. And the southern evangelical knew that even Satan could quote scripture, and decided that abolitionists were merely malefactors trying to make the teachings of Jesus conform to their own infidel philosophy.[157]

All exegetical interpreters were doing, simply put, was appealing to Thomas Thompson's argument against radical abolitionism from a hundred years prior: "open the Bible, read it, believe it."[158] The abolitionists on the other hand, were trying to appeal to something they deemed nobler, attempting to become "more merciful than God himself . . . affecting a philanthropy more pure and all embracing than that of Jesus Christ."[159] They were in effect, "trampling the Constitution and the Bible alike under their feet," while they "impiously appeal[ed] to a higher law than is found in either, to sanction their enormities."[160] Noll concludes, "The primary reason that the biblical defense of slavery remained so strong was that many biblical attacks on slavery were so weak."[161]

---

[157] Crowther, *Southern Evangelicals and the Coming of the Civil War*, 97.

[158] Noll, *The Civil War as a Theological Crisis*, 33.

[159] J.R. McKivigan and M. Snay, *Religion and the Antebellum Debate Over Slavery* (University of Georgia Press, 1998), 319.

[160] W.B. Cisco, *Wade Hampton: Confederate Warrior, Conservative Statesman* (Brassey's, 2004), 48.

[161] *Ibid.*, 40.

CHAPTER 4
BE YE SEPARATE

IN THE DECADE PRECEDING the War Between the States the tone of the debate changed from one of reasoned discussion to one of utter castigation. One might say it was the Northern abolitionists who started such rhetoric in 1831 when the immediate emancipators rose up in force,[162] but by the 1850s, many Southerners were matching abolitionist denunciations of the South with denunciations of their own. As early as directly proceeding 1830, John Blassingame tells us, "the rising tide of threats against and mob attacks on antislavery ministers made the clergy more cautious. The more outspoken critics abandoned their Southern pulpits for Northern ones."[163] In a letter featured in the *Presbyterian Witness of Knoxville* in 1856, Rev. Dr. Frederick A. Ross - an advocate of compensated emancipation[164] - denounced abolitionists with these words:

---

[162] Crowther, *Southern Evangelicals and the Coming of the Civil War*, 71.

[163] Blassingame, *The Slave Community*, 81.

[164] Compensated emancipation was the idea that the slaves ought to be freed, but if it was to happen immediately it was to be done in such a way that the slave owner is compensated for his slaves, an investment he would not be getting a return on. Otherwise, if all slaves were to be freed at once it would devastate the economy for white and black alike.

Ye men of Boston, New York, London, Paris – Ye Hypocrites – Ye brand me as a pirate, a kidnapper, a murderer, a demon fit only for hell ... Ye gabble about the sin of slavery, and then bow down to me, and buy and spin cotton, and thus work for me as truly as my slaves! O ye fools and blind, fill ye up the measure of your folly, and blindness, and shame! And this ye are doing. Ye have, like the French infidels, made reason your goddess, and are exalting her above the Bible; and, in your unitarianism and neology and all modes of infidelity, ye are rejecting and crucifying the Son of God.[165]

Whether this type of language was justified or not, it was certainly becoming more common as Southerners became completely outraged over abolitionist intrusions into their daily lives.

Religious Politics vs. Political Religion

It is worth remembering that Southern people had a much different view on the responsibility of government than their Northern counterparts did. First and foremost, Southerners were inclined toward divine command. A Methodist editorial noted that "government, or civil control, regulated by law, had its origins invariably in superior force, rather than in unanimity of opinion on the part of the subjects of government."[166] In an 1861 sermon, James Henley Thornwell stated: "Civil government is an institute of heaven, founded in the character of man as social and moral, and is

---

[165] F.A. Ross, *Slavery Ordained of God* (J.B. Lippincott & Co., 1857), 76-77.
[166] Crowther, *Evangelicals and the Coming of the Civil War*, 82.

designed to realise the idea of justice . . . As the state is essentially moral in its idea, it connects itself directly with the government of God."[167] Presbyterian preacher Thomas Smythe told his congregation in the preceding year that:

> To make it [the pulpit] the means of instructing Christians in the Christianity of their political relations, is simply to accomplish one of the ends for which it was intended. The same may be said of the religious press. The connection between true religion and sound politics is very intimate. The well-being of the one is the well-being of the other; the corruption of the one is the corruption of the other; the decay or the revival of the one is the decay or the revival of the other; and it is therefore proper that the public mind, in its political aspirations, should be brought under the influence of those principles which alone can rectify political opinion.[168]

Though the ministers of the South were fully aware of their duty before God to teach their flocks how to be politically involved in a Christian manner, they likewise understood that the government's responsibility before God occupied a wholly separate jurisdiction. This is why Smyth mixed his political comments regarding the necessity of the pulpit with the warning: "To convert the pulpit into an instrument of political agitation is most certainly to invade its sacredness; and they who do so, seldom fail to reap in

---

[167] F. Moore, *The Rebellion Record, Supplement* (Putnam, 1861), 56.

[168] An Association of Ministers in the Town of Columbia, S.C., "National Righteousness," *Southern Presbyterian Review* XII (1860), 25.

disappointment the fruits of their indiscretion."[169] This doctrine of spheres of authority allowed the Presbyterian synods of South Carolina and Georgia to affirm, at their December 1834 meeting, that "slavery is a political institution, with which the Church has nothing to do, except to inculcate the duties of master and slave, and to use lawful and spiritual means to have all, both bond and free, to become one in Christ by faith."[170]

Southern clergymen therefore "did not endorse candidates for office, but in the exercise of discussing biblical text or providing Southerners with moral instruction, they inculcated their audiences with definite notions about government."[171] Hence, it wasn't only the fact that religious abolitionists went beyond biblical authority that bothered Southern clergymen. It was also the fact that the North had confused the responsibility of the church with the responsibility of the state. A sizable consensus of Southern ministers "regard[ed] abolitionism as an interference with the plans of Divine Providence."[172] Quoting from *1 Timothy* 1-5, which encourages Christians to separate themselves from those who teach not in accord with Scripture, the Southerners declared, "This is what we teach and obedient to the last verse of the text, from men that 'teach otherwise' – hoping for peace – we 'withdraw' ourselves."[173] Thus,

---

[169] *Ibid*.

[170] G. Thompson and R.J. Breckinridge, *Discussion on American Slavery*, (I. Knapp, 1836), 76.

[171] Crowther, *Southern Evangelicals and the Coming of the Civil War*, 82.

[172] Conference of Ministers, Assembled at Richmond, Va., *An Address to Christians Throughout the World* (Parrish & Willingham, 1863), 8.

[173] *Ibid*.

when a modern student of history asks the question, "Why were not the Southern pulpits endeavoring through political means to eradicate slavery as their Northern counterparts were?" the answer is because of their position on government, not slavery. Even if individual Southern preachers did feel so inclined they would not have thought it their duty to leave their sphere of authority for one to which they held no jurisdiction. The abolitionists, as we have seen and will see, did not harbor any sympathy with this position.

INVASION OF THE ABOLITIONISTS

It is important to recognize, however unified their goal, that Northern Abolitionism was essentially comprised of two wings – an evangelical and non-evangelical. The evangelical wing consisted of Arminians inspired by Charles Finney and his perfectionism[174] while the non-evangelical wing was made up of the more potent Unitarian, Transcendentalist, and Quaker affiliations. While there did exist a significant amount of overlap, the evangelical prerogative was mainly harnessed in the form of mission efforts in the South, and the non-evangelical endeavors were more directed toward the publication of a myriad of abolitionist newspapers and the promotion of slave insurrections. Let us now explore how abolitionist beliefs were practically imposed on the South in the years preceding the war.

The Congregationalist-turned-atheist Elizur Wright, an editor for many abolitionist publications, stated in 1833 that "It is the duty of all men . . . to urge upon slaveholders immediate emancipation,

---

[174] Singer, *A Theological Interpretation of American History*, 74.

so long as there is a slave – to agitate the consciences of tyrants, so long as there is a tyrant on the globe."[175] The most outspoken and famous "agitator" was Transcendentalist William Lloyd Garrison's newspaper *The Liberator* which ran from 1831 until the end of the war. "The cry of . . . Garrison that slavery was a crime and the slave holders were criminals" put the South on a firmly defensive footing.[176] Frank Lawrence Owsley gives us a more specific look into the rhetoric contained within the publication's pages.

> The slave master, said Garrison, debauched his women slaves, had children by them, and in turn defiled his own children and sold them into the slave market; the slave plantation was primarily a gigantic harem for the master and his sons . . . Ministers of the gospel who owned or sanctioned slavery were included in his sweeping indictment of miscegenation and prostitution. In short, Garrison and the anti-slavery societies which he launched, followed soon by Northern churchman, stigmatized the South as a black brothel . . . They [slave owners] were cruel and brooding tyrants, who drove their slaves till they dropped and died, who starved them to save food, let them go cold and almost naked to save clothing, let them dwell in filthy pole pens rather than build them comfortable cottages, beat them unmercifully with leather thongs filled with spikes, dragged cats over their bodies and faces, trailed them with bloodhounds which rent and chewed

---

[175] B. Lundy, *Genius of Universal Emancipation* (B. Lundy, 1833), 186.
[176] Twelve Southerners, *I'll Take My Stand*, 79.

them, – then sprinkled their wounds with salt and red pepper. Infants were torn from their mothers' breasts and sold to Simon Legrees [slave trader from *Uncle Tom's Cabin*]; families were separated and scattered to the four winds . . . Such charges, printed in millions upon millions of pamphlets, were sent out all over the world. Sooner or later, much of it was accepted as true in the North.[177]

This, despite the fact that Garrison "was completely ignorant of the South and of negro slavery."[178]

It was radicals like Garrison who absolutely horrified the South. The law itself had no restraint on their mission – a mission willing to use any means possible as exemplified in the case of John Brown. Jefferson Davis and other Southerners harbored "great offense" at abolitionist William H. Seward's comment that there existed a "higher law than the Constitution"[179] rooted in a Creator who remained, practically speaking, unrevealed in the pages of Scripture. Garrison even "had the courage to publicly burn the Constitution for its tolerance of slavery"[180] calling it a "covenant with Death" and "agreement with Hell."[181]

---

[177] *Ibid.*, 79-80.

[178] *Ibid.*, 79.

[179] Stephen A. Douglas *et al.*, *The Nebraska Question* (Redfield, 1854), 27.

[180] J.B. Stewart, *William Lloyd Garrison at Two Hundred: History, Legacy, and Memory* (Yale University Press, 2008), 121.

[181] J.J. Chapman, *William Lloyd Garrison* (Moffat, Yard and Co., 1913), 172.

It looked like, from the Southern point of view, that whether it came to the Fugitive Slave Act, the Dred Scott decision, or the right to take slaves into the territories, whenever Yankees lost they criticized the rules. Charleston minister Thomas Smyth surmised: "They have a zeal of God, but it is not according to knowledge . . . They substitute opinion for truth, dogmatism for doctrine, philosophy (falsely so called) for religion; and, adopting as a maxim the jesuitical dogma that the end sanctifies the means, they stop at nothing."[182] It would have been one thing if such rhetoric was never practically applied, but time proved otherwise. After the death of the terrorist John Brown, who had attempted to start a slave insurrection at Harper's Ferry with the funding of at least six wealthy and prominent abolitionists, Garrison had the nerve to offer him a martyr's eulogy.[183] Unitarian minister Ralph Waldo Emerson went further by stating that when the abolitionist/terrorist John Brown was hanged he would "make the gallows as glorious as the cross."[184] Julia Ward Howe, also a Unitarian and author of the "Battle Hymn of the Republic," referred to John Brown as "a very noble man, who should be in one of the many mansions of which Christ tells us."[185] The South was appalled. Here was a convicted murderer being hailed by abolitionists as a messianic figure.

---

[182] Thomas Smyth, "The War of the South Vindicated," *The Southern Presbyterian Review* XV, No. 4 (April 1863), 480.

[183] L. Copeland, L.W. Lamm, and S.J. McKenna, *The World's Great Speeches* (Dover Publications, 1999), 299-301.

[184] S.D. Carpenter, *Logic of History* (S.D. Carpenter, 1864), 69.

[185] L.E.H. Richards, M.H. Elliott, and F.H. Hall, *Julia Ward Howe, 1819-1910* (Houghton Mifflin Co., 1915), 179.

It didn't help things any that slave insurrections had always been a fear among many in the South. Thomas Jefferson "toyed with the idea of gradual emancipation" until the Haitian rebellion which hardened him against it.[186] Nat Turner's 1831 rebellion in Virginia, which killed more than 100 people, mostly children, was a very interesting case. Turner had a kind master, the ability to read, and became a Baptist preacher.[187] Unfortunately, he "felt inspired by a vision to kill every white person he could find."[188] Historian J.W. Blassingame tells us that:

> Although information is limited, it is possible to draw a portrait of the antebellum black rebel leaders. For the most part, they were young, literate, married, charismatic men. Finding sanctions for their bloodletting in the Bible, inspiring the faint-hearted with apocalyptic visions from the Scriptures of God delivering the Israelites from the hands of their oppressors, the leaders convinced the blacks that slavery was contrary to the will of God and that He commanded them to rise.[189]

It was right after Turner's rebellion, when the Virginia legislature had been on the brink of enacting a plan to free and

---

[186] Crocker, *The Politically Incorrect Guide to the Civil War* (Regnery Pub., 2008), 23.

[187] *Ibid.*, 23-24.

[188] *Ibid.*, 24.

[189] Blassingame, *The Slave Community*, 221. As in the Denmark Vesey failed insurrection in Charleston, the leaders also used African voodoo to motivate their followers.

deport slaves, that instead, a law was passed barring slaves from receiving an education "so that they could not preach an unholy gospel, as Turner had done."[190] Though this law was widely ignored, most notably by Thomas J. "Stonewall" Jackson, who ran a Sunday school for both slave and free blacks, teaching them to read and write,[191] it only poured fuel on the fire by giving ammunition to abolitionists who criticized the law. Still, may Southerners in the wake of Brown's raid had vocalized their faith in the loyalty of the slaves given their unwillingness to join the uprising.[192] One North Carolina Presbyterian stated, "As a class, they [slaves] are faithful, generous, and affectionate, and their attachment to their masters is above suspicion."[193] History has somewhat vindicated this view considering the lack of slave uprisings during the war when men were not on their plantations to maintain order. Therefore, it wasn't so much slaves themselves that the white Southerners mistrusted. It was more so Northern abolitionist's ability to stir them up. "Turner and Brown helped convince Southerners that they had no friends in the North."[194] Thus, the fear of a "slave uprising" – especially a Northern-instigated one – was a common topic of discussion within the Davis presidency.[195]

---

[190] Crocker, *The Politically Incorrect Guide to the Civil War*, 23.

[191] *Ibid.*, 24.

[192] Crowther, *Evangelicals and the Coming of the Civil War*, 176.

[193] *Ibid.*

[194] Crocker, *The Politically Incorrect Guide to the Civil War*, 24.

[195] *The Papers of Jefferson Davis: 1862* (Louisiana State University Press, 1995), 143, 197, 263, 346, 516.

While evangelical abolitionists, in contrast to their more secular comrades, were orthodox in their language about God, their basic theology was not really all that different and neither was their rhetoric. Wesleyan missionary Daniel Wilson believed the South to be the "land of whips & chains & mobs,"[196] while his colleague Jesse McBride maintained that "slaveholders could not be Christians nor gain salvation."[197] In fact, "Horse thieves," he said, "were angels compared to them."[198] AMA missionary John C. Richardson threatened Southerners by claiming, falsely, "there are 40 thousand [blacks] in Canada training daily and they will come down here & cut your throats." (The comment incited a Kentucky mob to form, but no violence occurred.)[199]

One of the key differences that set evangelical abolitionists apart was a rigid legalism that foreshadowed the fundamentalist movement. "Economic exploitation, sexual license, gambling, drinking and dueling, disregard for family ties – all traits associated with slave-owning – could easily be set in bold contrast with the pure ideals of Yankee evangelicalism."[200] "Northern evangelicals simply had to ensure that its citizens became good Christians and that residual evil customs and corrupt social systems, like slavery and drunkenness, were eliminated. To realize its mission as a righteous republic, the United States could no longer sanction

---

[196] Harrold, *The Abolitionists and the South*, 93.

[197] *Ibid.*, 94.

[198] *Ibid.*

[199] V.B. Howard, *The Evangelical War Against Slavery and Caste: The Life and Times of John G. Fee* (Susquehanna University Press, 1996), 104.

[200] Stewart, *Holy Warriors*, 42-43.

slavery."[201] The doctrine of decisional regeneration – a doctrine not characteristic of Southern evangelicalism[202] – was carried into every facet of life. It was essentially a "social gospel" that looked to both the church and government to enact its reforms on individuals. "Thornwell, Dabney, and their contemporaries" rightly "saw in abolitionism a threat to Calvinism, to the Constitution, and to the proper ordering of society."[203]

One can only wonder what the outcome would have been if the evangelical abolitionists kept their movement contained in the north where it wouldn't have affected the Southern Calvinists. However, this is not at all what happened.

In 1839, Massachusetts minister Charles T. Torrey, in a letter to another reverend asked,

> What say you to a New Missionary Society, to 'evangelize the slaveholders' and their slaves? whose missionaries shall preach that 'the laborer is worthy of his hire?' ... who shall in spite of slavery and its bloody laws, teach the slaves to read the Bible, and then put Bibles and tracts into their hands."[204]

Such an idea attempted to harness the gospel in an attempt to "overthrow slavery," as fellow abolitionist and pastor Joshua

---

[201] Crowther, *Southern Evangelicals and the Coming of the Civil War*, 8.
[202] *Ibid.*, 42.
[203] Singer, *A Theological Interpretation of American History*, 86.
[204] J.C. Lovejoy, *Memoir of Rev. Charles T. Torrey* (J.P. Jewett & Co., 1847), 68.

Leavitt proclaimed.[205] By the late 1840s, Torrey's call was answered when the "the American Wesleyan Connection, the AMA [American Mission Association], and the American Baptist Free Missionary Society (ABFMS) each initiated measures to spread antislavery religion in the South"[206] and abstain from Christian fellowship with slave-owners and their churches.[207] Their goal, in the words of the Wesleyan abolitionist Luther Lee, was:

> to send anti-slavery missionaries to the south, or aid in supporting those whom God in his providence may rise up in that land of whips and chains and gags, to preach deliverance to the captives, and the opening of the prison door to them that are bound.[208]

Such organizations were typically comprised of missionaries characterized by being young, influenced by Finney's millennial theology, primarily from the North – especially the famous Burned-over district of New York – and many were Oberlin students.[209] Oberlin College in Ohio – whose president was Charles Finney – became a major driving force behind abolitionism's "missions" movement.

After Theodore Weld, one of Finney's protégés, incited an 1834 student revolt at Cincinnati's Lane Seminary in favor of immediate

---

[205] Harrold, *The Abolitionists and the South*, 85.
[206] *Ibid.*
[207] *Ibid.*, 87.
[208] *Ibid.*, 88.
[209] *Ibid.*, 90.

abolitionism,[210] the administration attempted to "[suppress] the Students' Anti-Slavery league, and in consequence 51 students left Lane and went to Oberlin,"[211] making it the educational "center of abolitionism."[212] Oberlin thus became the factory producing emissaries of the abolitionist gospel – a gospel wholly different than what Southerners were used to.

There is no doubt the gospel preached by the evangelical abolitionists was not the traditional gospel of orthodox Christianity. The American and Foreign Anti-Slavery Society (AFASS) declared in 1850, upon hearing of the success of Rev. John G. Fee in forming an anti-slavery church in Kentucky, "[It] shows that the Gospel can be thus preached in slave States."[213] In the words of historian Stanley Harrold:

> This was not the gospel preached regularly in the South or in much of the North. From the 1830s onward, abolitionists denounced what they called a proslavery gospel that either ignored the issue of slavery or actively denied that Christian principles favored emancipation. In contrast, they preached what they called a 'whole,' 'pure,' or 'free,' gospel, emphasizing Bible precepts that non-abolitionists avoided.[214]

---

[210] *Ibid.*, 56.
[211] L.F. Post, *The Public* (Louis F. Post, 1901), 807.
[212] Harrold, *The Abolitionists and the South*, 90.
[213] *Ibid.*, 89.
[214] *Ibid.*, 92-93.

One missionary expressed his intention "to go to the far South, to pronounce that Gospel which proclaims liberty to the captive, and the opening of the prison to them that are bound."[215] To Southerners, it was sin that Christ freed humanity from, not physical slavery. The evangelical abolitionists were so intent on their erroneous definition of the Gospel that they maintained non-slaveholders who attended churches with congregations partially comprised of slaveholders, were in sin.[216]

Lest someone think that the evangelical abolitionists were simply just trying to recruit Southerners to the power of their arguments, let us examine the testimony of one slaveholder in North Carolina who told missionary Jesse McBride, "You have ruined my slaves; I can't do a thing with them."[217] Hence, their mission was more than winning a debate and progressively changing a community – it was built on the idea of incitement. "[They] knew that their efforts depended on agitation for success. They designed their churches . . . to provoke dissension in neighboring congregations and to develop a corps of come-outers."[218] The missionaries would target slaves, attempt to get them into their churches, and then preach their right to be free, essentially encouraging them to disobey or escape from their masters.[219]

---

[215] *Ibid.*, 93.
[216] *Ibid.*, 94.
[217] *Ibid.*, 97.
[218] *Ibid.*, 97.
[219] *Ibid.*, 93, 99.

One missionary saw himself as "excit[ing] the slaves" in the same way that "Moses and Aaron excited the minds of the oppressed Hebrews."[220] Of course, "knocking on doors" and running church services was not all they did. Literature distribution was perhaps the main weapon used to stir up dissension. In 1835, mass abolitionist mailings to the South, referred to as the "postal crisis," served as the first step in getting Southern ministers involved in the immediate abolition debate.[221] Again from 1843 to 1861 Northern antislavery publications flooded the South.[222] One missionary estimated that by 1859 "twenty millions of tracts" had been distributed,[223] this time causing a colder reaction mainly due to the fact that many AMA missionaries were simultaneously actively assisting slaves in escaping their masters (recall the fear Southerners harbored of a "slave revolt"). Such "agitators" were increasingly being mobbed, jailed, and forced to leave Southern states.[224]

DENOMINATION FRAGMENTATION

As hopefully the reader is already aware, the unorthodox of the North did not acknowledge their own deviation. Unitarians, Transcendentalists, Quakers, Wesleyans, and the Northern denominational factions legitimately thought they were doing the

---

[220] *Ibid.*, 103.
[221] Crowther, *Southern Evangelicals and the Coming of the Civil War*, 71.
[222] Harrold, *The Abolitionists and the South*, 95.
[223] *Ibid.*, 95.
[224] *Ibid.*, 99-101.

will of God as communicated to them through conscience and personal conviction. What they were not doing however was interpreting the Word of God according to language and history. Any time the Scriptures were used to support radical abolitionism they were eisegesically rendered. This line of thinking did not invade overnight in one fell swoop. It took time – denomination by denomination.

The Presbyterians were the first major denomination to divide in 1837 right after the "postal crisis." In 1787, the denomination had maintained that while slavery wasn't necessarily a sin, it was acknowledged that one day when "Providence shall open the way for it'" slaves would hopefully be set free.[225] Because of the South's view on civil government, as already mentioned, the denomination did not take any political stand other than affirming, by 1830, that "ministers to negroes wouldn't focus on [their] civil condition."[226] However, after the threat of immediate emancipation arose in the early 1830s accompanied by Nat Turner's revolt and the "postal crisis," Southerners became highly defensive of the slave system. The synod of South Carolina affirmed that:

> Slavery had existed from the days of those good old slaveholders and patriots, Abraham, Isaac, and Jacob; that the existence of slavery is not opposed to the will of God, and [that] whosoever has a conscience too tender to recognize this relation as lawful, is righteous over much, is

---

[225] *Journal of Presbyterian History* (Presbyterian Historical Society, 1902), 217-218.
[226] Ibid., 70.

wise above what is written . . . and leaves the infallible word of God for the fancies and doctrine of men.[227]

Right before the great schism, James Smylie, clerk of the Mississippi Presbytery, got into a public debate with Gerrit Smith, who was a prominent abolitionist and member of the "secret six" who financed John Brown. While Smylie did affirm the fact that slavery could potentially be a sin if practiced unbiblically, he made known the South's position when he quipped, "The proper relation [of slave to master] is not charged with evils any more than marriage is charged with adultery."[228] At the time however their existed many "New School" Presbyterians who could not accept this, and while the "division was not entirely along abolitionist and pro-slavery lines, one group [New School] drew to its ranks a preponderance of the Church's abolitionists while the other [Old School] found its strength in the anti-abolitionist faction."[229] Historian Gregg Singer notes:

> After 1840 [Old School Presbyterians] . . . took a very strong stand against Abolitionism as a movement, not because it was opposed to slavery per se, but because of the philosophy and theology which it represented, and because they clearly saw that if this radicalism were to gain the supremacy in the national government, then there must certainly come in its wake a radical political and social

---

[227] Crowther, *Southern Evangelicals and the Coming of the Civil War*, 72.

[228] *Ibid.*, 73.

[229] Bruce C. Staiger, "Abolitionism and the Presbyterian Schism of 1837-1838," *Mississippi Valley Historical Review* (1949), 391.

program which would threaten the established order and constitutional government for the nation as a whole.[230]

The 1837 schism was only partially over abolitionism-- it was mainly over the 1801 Plan of Union between Congregationalists – influenced by Transcendentalism – and New School Presbyterians to do joint missions work in the Ohio Valley[231]. In 1857 and 1861, both Northern and Southern wings of the Old and New School denominations split within themselves. However, this time it was entirely over the issue.

In the *Book of Discipline*, which codified the religious duties of the Methodists, slavery was said to be a "great evil." However, at the 1816 general conference it was "ruled that Methodists who resided in states where emancipation was illegal or fraught with hardships for the manumitted slaves were not bound by the Discipline's anti-slavery dicta."[232] Slaveholders like William Capers and Evan W. Winans were able to work within this system,[233] that is, until 1836 when Northerners showed their lack of approval for electing Capers to the position of bishop simply because he owned slaves.[234] The following year Capers still called for unity within the denomination despite what had happened. He wrote in the *Southern Christian Advocate*:

---

[230] Singer, *A Theological Interpretation of the United States*, 84.
[231] *Ibid.*, 81.
[232] Crowther, *Southern Evangelicals and the Coming of the Civil War*, 62.
[233] *Ibid.*, 62-63.
[234] *Ibid.*, 65.

> In the present state of the country, we believe it to be of the utmost importance to the country itself that the churches be kept together. Let the bonds once be severed which hold the churches of the North and South together and the Union of these states will be more than endangered, it will presently be rent asunder.[235]

In effect, Capers had just predicted the War Between the States. Regrettably, not everyone shared his mediating spirit. William A. Smith called for a new denomination in light of Capers's mistreatment,[236] a call which would be answered less than a decade later. First, the Wesleyan Church broke off in 1843 denouncing slaveholding as intrinsically sinful and becoming the main driving force behind abolitionist efforts in the South from 1847 onward.[237] The next year, when Bishop James Osgood Andrew received slaves by marriage without freeing them, Northern Methodists called for his suspension though his actions did not violate any Methodist statute. As a result, William Capers and a band of Southerners seceded from the denomination to form their own. By this time Capers attitude had changed significantly. He exclaimed, "We denounce the principles and opinions of the abolitionists *in toto* . . .

---

[235] C.C. Goen, *Broken Churches, Broken Nation: Denominational Schisms and the Coming of the American Civil War* (Mercer University Press, 1985), 81.

[236] *Ibid.*

[237] Harrold, *The Abolitionists and the South*, 87.

We consider and believe that the Holy Scriptures . . . do unequivocally authorize the relation of master and slave."[238]

The fragmentation of the Baptist church resembles the Methodist schism quite a bit. Both were over the same issue – the North's dismissal of slaveholding members – and both occurred in the same year. Just like Methodists and Presbyterians, most Baptists in the late 1700s generally viewed slavery as a political issue and not a religious one. They taught the biblical responsibilities of slaves to masters and masters to slaves.[239] In 1822, a freed slave by the name of Denmark Vesey attempted to instigate murder of whites in Charleston and instigate a revolt. One slave later testified that "he studied the Bible a great deal and tried to prove from it that slavery and bondage is against the Bible."[240] In the wake of this failed attempt the president of the Baptist State Convention of South Carolina, Dr. Richard Furman, assured the governor that:

> The Convention are particularly unhappy in considering, that an idea of the Bible's teaching the doctrine of emancipation as necessary, and tending to make servants insubordinate to proper authority, has obtained access to any mind . . . Several of these [Vesey's followers] were grossly immoral, and, in general, they were members of an irregular body, which called itself the African Church, and

---

[238] G. Thompson and R.J. Breckinridge, *Report of the Discussion on American Slavery* (D. Prentice & Co., 1836), 91-92.

[239] Crowther, *Southern Evangelicals and the Coming of the Civil War*, 65.

[240] J.H. Franklin and A.A. Moss, *From Slavery to Freedom: A History of African Americans* (Knopf, 1994), 141.

had intimate connections and intercourse with a similar body of men in a Northern City, among whom the supposed right to emancipation is strenuously advocated.[241]

Thus distancing Baptists from any participation in radical abolitionism, Furman affirmed the biblical teaching:

> Had the holding of slaves been a moral evil, it cannot be supposed, that the inspired Apostles . . . would have tolerated it, for a moment, in the Christian Church . . . They would have . . . required, that the master should liberate his slave in the first instance. But, instead of this, they let the relationship remain untouched, as being lawful and right, and insist on the relative duties.[242]

As the abolitionist threat became more and more potent, other groups of Baptists from the South became outspoken. The Alabama Baptist convention of 1835 maintained that:

> . . . certain individuals, mostly residing in the Northern part of the United States, calling themselves abolitionists, but who are properly called . . . fanatics, have formed themselves into societies, for the purpose of interfering with the relation of master and slaves. Their activities were "inconsistent with the gospel of Christ." Abolitionists will "oppress the slave, . . . arm the assassin to shed the blood

---

[241] J.R. Young, *Proslavery and Sectional Thought in the Early South, 1740-1829: An Anthology* (University of South Carolina Press, 2006), 235-236.
[242] *Ibid.*, 231.

of the good people of our State; and . . . alienate the people in one State from those in another, thereby endangering the peace and permanency of our happy Republic."[243]

Mississippi Baptists likewise denounced in 1837 "the movement of the abolitionists at the North [as] . . . misguided and impolitic, and . . . calculated . . . to detract from the social, civil, and religious privileges of the slave population."[244]

When missionaries James Huckins and William Tyron were found to be slaveholders in 1843, anti-slavery Baptists demanded the Triennial Convention board investigate them.[245] By 1844, the battle lines between the North and South were firmly drawn at the triennial gathering of the American Baptist Missionary Union where James Reeve was denied entry to the national board for owning slaves based upon the view that missionaries had to manumit slaves before being accepted.[246] It was this action that precipitated Georgians and Virginians to establish the Southern Baptist Convention the following year.[247] At this point the Great Lakes Region Baptists had already formed an abolitionist convention.[248] Now it was the South's turn to start their own decidedly anti-

---

[243] Crowther, *Southern Evangelicals and the Coming of the Civil War*, 74.
[244] Ibid., 74.
[245] Ibid.
[246] Ibid.
[247] Noll, *The Civil War as a Theological Crisis*, 36.
[248] Ibid.

abolitionist denomination, one which would value Scripture over sentiment and theology over politics.

In a speech given in Augusta, Georgia in 1845 on the origin of the new convention, William B. Johnson, the first president of the Southern Baptist Convention, expressed his reluctance to separate, calling the division "painful."[249] After expressing a common bond in the "principles of the gospel,"[250] and an unwillingness to exclude those of like faith in the North, as many Southerners had been excluded, Johnson laid out the reasons for the departure claiming that the missionary board in Boston had "thus acted upon a sentiment they have failed to prove—That slavery is, in all circumstances, sinful."[251] Johnson demonstrated that the board was not only in violation of Scripture, but also of the Constitution of the General Convention for usurping the Convention's authority to define the qualifications for being a missionary. Furthermore, the missionary board also violated the Convention's resolution that specifically allowed for the expression and promotion of views on the subject of slavery as long as such views were communicated in a "Christian manner and spirit."[252] The missionary board made the relinquishing of such speech a requirement in order to serve.

---

[249] John R. Bigelow, *The Baptist Memorial and Monthly Record.* v. 4., 1845. 219.

[250] *Ibid.*

[251] *Ibid.*, 220.

[252] *Ibid.*

Emphatically, Johnson twice cited 1 Thess 2:16, "They would forbid us to speak unto the gentiles,"[253] as the main reason for the schism.

> "We can never be a party to any arrangement" for monopolizing the Gospel: any arrangement which like that of the Autocratical Interdict of the North, would first drive us from our beloved colored people, of whom they prove that they know nothing comparatively, and from the much-wronged Aborigines of the country; and then cut us off from the whitening fields of the heathen harvest-labor."[254]

In an emotional ending Johnson refers to his Northern counterparts as, "beloved brethren and old co-adjutors in this cause [of world missions]."[255] He sets the goal for the new denomination to extend the Messiah's kingdom and the glory of God until "the deserts of unconverted human nature 'rejoice and blossom as the rose.'"[256]

And with firm resolution the Southern Baptist denomination was born, perhaps many of its leaders knowing deep down this would not be the first time they would be called to separate from the North.

---

[253] *Ibid.*, 254.
[254] *Ibid.*, 221.
[255] *Ibid.*, 222.
[256] *Ibid.*

Conclusion

THE CAUSES THAT LEAD to the "American Civil War" were not simply between abolitionists and slave-owners, nationalists and Constitutionaliststs, Republicans and Democrats, or capitalists and socialists. The war was over something much more profound. It was a divorce encouraged by religious differences between eisegetical interpreters and exegetical interpreters, between autonomists and those holding to "Thus saith the Lord," between humanists and Calvinists, between earthly utopia and the promise of heaven.

The war came down to a fight over two visions of reality – the world in which man creates an earthly paradise on one hand, or the world in which men await a heavenly reward on the other. This is the major error of humanism – that heaven awaits us in this world. Though its ideas seem to be morally upright, especially when beaming in the robe of abolition, the history of both the 20th and 21st centuries have proven otherwise, as man has unhinged himself from every social obligation and heavenly restraint. The promise of freedom turns into a different kind of bondage, more terrible than the one previously erased.

Like the critics of Southern Christians in the mid-19th century, today's religious social justice warriors must also compromise *sola scriptura* or exegetical interpretation to make their case. The progressive's hope, "Our Father who art in Washington" whose mission is to widen democracy and dispel inequity does little, if anything, to improve the condition of the marginalized -even if theoretically it improves their political status. One only need consider the failures of the welfare state and successes of the decentralized pro-life movement.

Once the authority of God's word is deserted, there is no standard left governing man's behavior. Such thinking will never lead to a perfect society. Utopia will have to wait. In the words of James Henley Thornwell "[It is when] we are prone to feel ourselves at home in this world when things go smoothly, that the Lord finds it necessary to cross us and disappoint us, in order that we may know that this is not our rest."[257] The Christian as well as the true Southerner knows that there is only one source of rest on this earth, and it is not to be found in the material, but in the spiritual. As the Master of all has told us, it is those who find their faith, not in government or social organization that truly find peace, but those who flee to Him. "Come to Me, all who are weary and heavy-laden, and I will give you rest."[258] It is in the authority of these words, and those that come before and after them, that Southerners found their sacred conviction. May these words be true for you as well.

---

[257] Crowther, *Southern Evangelicals and the Coming of the Civil War*, 30.

[258] *Matthew* 11:28 (New American Standard Bible).

Bibliography

American Journal of Education, 1865.

An Association of Ministers in the Town of Columbia, S.C. "National Righteousness." *Southern Presbyterian Review* XII (1860).

———. *Southern Presbyterian Review* I, no. I (June 1847).

Ayers, Edward. *American Passages: A History of the United States.* 4th ed. Boston, Mass.: Wadsworth/Cengage Learning, 2009.

Bacon, L. *Slavery Discussed in Occasional Essays, from 1833 to 1846.* Baker and Scribner, 1846.

Barnes, A. *The Church and Slavery.* Negro Universities Press, 1857.

Bensel, R.F. *Yankee Leviathan: The Origins of Central State Authority in America,* 1859-1877. Cambridge University Press, 1990.

Bigelow, John R., *The Baptist Memorial and Monthly Record.* v. 4., 1845. 219.

Blanchard, J., and N.L. Rice. *A Debate on Slavery.* W.H. Moore & Co., 1846.

Blassingame, J.W. *The Slave Community: Plantation Life in the Antebellum South.* Oxford University Press, 1979.

Blumenfeld, S.L. *Is Public Education Necessary?* Devin-Adair Co., 1981.

———. "How Harvard Went from Calvinism to Unitarianism," *The New American.* [thenewamerican.com] March 1, 2011.

Buckingham, J.S. *The Slave States of America*, Fisher, Son & Co., 1842.

Burton, O.V. *The Age of Lincoln*. Farrar, Straus and Giroux, 2008.

Carey, Matthew Jr. *The Democratic Speaker's Hand-Book: Containing Every Thing Necessary for the Defense of the National Democracy in the Coming Presidential Campaign, and for the Assault of the Radical Enemies of the Country and its Constitution*. Cincinnati, Ohio: Miami Print. and Pub. Co., 1868.

Carpenter, S.D. *Logic of History*. S.D. Carpenter, 1864.

Cash, W.J. *The Mind of the South*. Vintage Books, 1991.

Cave, R.C. *The Men in Gray*. Confederate Veteran, 1911.

Chaplain J. Wm. Jones. "The Inner Life of Robert Edward Lee." *The Chautauquan: A Magazine for Self-Education*, April 1900.

Chapman, J.J. *William Lloyd Garrison*. Moffat, Yard and Co., 1913.

Cisco, W.B. *Wade Hampton: Confederate Warrior, Conservative Statesman*. Brassey's, 2004.

Conference of Ministers, Assembled at Richmond, Va. *An Address to Christians Throughout the World*. Parrish & Willingham, 1863.

Constitution of the Confederate States.

Cooke, G.W. *Unitarianism in America: A History of its Origin and Development*. American Unitarian Association, 1902.

Copeland, L., L.W. Lamm, and S.J. McKenna. *The World's Great Speeches*. Dover Publications, 1999.

Cralle', Richard K. *The Works of John C. Calhoun*. Vol. IV. New York: D. Appleton and Company, 1854.

Crocker. *The Politically Incorrect Guide to the Civil War*. Regnery, 2008.

Croscup, G.E., and E.D. Lewis. *History Made Visible: A Synchronic Chart and Statistical Tables of United States History*. Windsor Pub. Co., 1910.

Crowther, Edward. *Southern Evangelicals and the Coming of the Civil War.* Lewiston, N.Y.: E. Mellen Press, 2000.

Dabney, R.L. *A Defence of Virginia: (And Through Her, of the South) in Recent and Pending Contests Against the Sectional Party.* E.J. Hale, 1867.

Davis, Jefferson. *The Papers of Jefferson Davis: 1862.* Louisiana State University Press, 1995.

Davis, Jefferson. *The Rise and Fall of the Confederate Government,* 1881.

DiLorenzo, T.J. *The Real Lincoln: A New Look at Abraham Lincoln, His Agenda, and an Unnecessary War.* Three Rivers Press, 2003.

Dorough, C. *The Bible Belt Mystique.* Philadelphia, Pa.: Westminster Press, 1974.

Douglas, Stephen A. et al. *The Nebraska Question.* Redfield, 1854.

Douglass, Frederick. *My Bondage and My Freedom.* Miller, Orton & Mulligan, 1855.

Duncan, J. *A Treatise on Slavery.* American Anti-Slavery Society, 1840.

Dyke, H.J.V. *The Character and Influence of Abolitionism.* H. Taylor, 1860.

Emerson, R.W. *The Complete Works of Ralph Waldo Emerson: The Conduct of Life.* Houghton, Mifflin, 1859.

Episcopal Church. Diocese of South Carolina. *Journal of the Proceedings of the Fifty-Fourth Annual Convention of the Protestant Episcopal Church, in South Carolina.* The Diocese, 1843.

Farrow, A.J. Lang, and J. Frank. *Complicity: How the North Promoted, Prolonged, and Profited from Slavery.* Random House, 2006.

Faust, D.G. *The Ideology of Slavery: Proslavery Thought in the Antebellum South, 1830-1860.* Louisiana State University Press, 1981.

Franklin, J.H. and A.A. Moss. *From Slavery to Freedom: A History of African Americans.* Knopf, 1994.

Gaustad, E.S. *A Religious History of America*. Harper & Row, 1966.

Goen, C.C. *Broken Churches, Broken Nation: Denominational Schisms and the Coming of the American Civil War*. Mercer University Press, 1985.

Grusin, Richard. *Transcendentalist Hermeneutics: Institutional Authority and the Higher Criticism of the Bible*. Duke University Press, 1991.

Harrold, S. *The Abolitionists and the South, 1831-1861*. University Press of Kentucky, 1999.

Himes, A. *The Sword of the Lord: The Roots of Fundamentalism in an American Family*. CreateSpace, 2010.

Holzer, H. *Lincoln at Cooper Union: The Speech That Made Abraham Lincoln President*. Simon & Schuster, 2006.

Howard, V.B. *The Evangelical War Against Slavery and Caste: The Life and Times of John G. Fee*. Susquehanna University Press, 1996.

Kennedy, James R. and Walter D. Kennedy. *Was Jefferson Davis Right?* Pelican Pub. Co., 1998.

Kennedy, Walter D. *Myths of American Slavery*. Pelican Pub. Co., 2003.

Kuklick, B., and D.G. Hart. *Religious Advocacy and American History*. W.B. Eerdmans Co., 1997.

Lauer, Paul E. *Church and State in New England*, II-III X. Baltimore: The Johns Hopkins Press, 1892.

Lincoln, A. *The Collected Works of Abraham Lincoln*. Wildside Press, 2008.

Littell, Franklin. *From State Church to Pluralism: A Protestant Interpretation of Religion in American History*. New Brunswick, N.J.: Transaction, 2007.

Lovejoy, J.C. *Memoir of Rev. Charles T. Torrey*. J.P. Jewett & Co., 1847.

Lundy, B. *Genius of Universal Emancipation*. B. Lundy, 1833.

"Management of Slaves." *The American Farmer*. Baltimore, September 1846.

McKivigan, J.R., and M. Snay. *Religion and the Antebellum Debate Over Slavery*. University of Georgia Press, 1998.

McTyeire, H.N., C.F. Sturgis, A.T. Holmes. *Duties of Masters to Servants: Three Premium Essays*. Southern Baptist Publication Society, 1851.

McTyeire, H.N., and T.O. Summers. *Duties of Christian Masters*. Southern Methodist Publishing House, 1859.

Meriwether, E.A. *Facts and Falsehoods Concerning the War on the South, 1861-1865*. A.R. Taylor & Co., 1904.

Moore, F. *The Rebellion Record, Supplement*. Putnam, 1864.

Mott, F.L. *A History of American Magazines, 1850-1865*. Harvard University Press, 1938.

Noll, Mark. *A History of Christianity in the United States and Canada*. Eerdmans, 1992.

_____. *The Civil War as a Theological Crisis*. University of North Carolina Press, 2006.

Owen, Christopher. *The Sacred Flame of Love: Methodism and Society in Nineteenth-Century Georgia*. University of Georgia Press, 1998.

Palmer, Benjamin.M.. *The Life and Letters of James Henley Thornwell*. Whittet & Shepperson, 1875.

_____. "Spirit of the Pulpit." *The Rebellion Record* XV, 1863.

Phillips, Wendell. *Speeches, Lectures, and Letters*. Boston, Mass.: James Redpath, 1863.

Pollard, E.A. *The Lost Cause: A New Southern History of the War of the Confederates*. E.B. Treat & Co., 1866.

"Population of the United States in 1860." Government Printing Office, 1864.

Post, L.F. *The Public.* Louis F. Post, 1901.

Presbyterian Historical Society, and Historical Foundation of the Presbyterian and Reformed Churches. *Journal of Presbyterian History.* Presbyterian Historical Society, 1902.

Richards, L.E.H., M.H. Elliott, and F.H. Hall. *Julia Ward Howe, 1819-1910.* Houghton Mifflin Co., 1915.

Robert Livingston Stanton, D.D. *The Church and the Rebellion: A Consideration of the Rebellion Against the Government of the United States; and the Agency of the Church, North and South, in Relation Thereto.* New York: Derby & Miller, 1864.

Ross, F.A. *Slavery Ordained of God.* J.B. Lippincott & Co., 1857

Rumburg, Rondel H. *Was Abraham Lincoln a Christian? A Debate.* Spout Spring: VA Society for Biblical and Southern Studies, 2006.

Schecter, B. *The Devil's Own Work: The Civil War Draft Riots and the Fight to Reconstruct America.* Walker & Company, 2007.

Singer, C. Gregg, *A Theological Interpretation of American History.* 2nd ed. Phillipsburg, N.J.: Presbyterian and Reformed Pub. Co., 1981.

Smith, C.P. *Yankees and God.* Hermitage House, 1954

Smyth, Thomas. "The War of the South Vindicated." *The Southern Presbyterian Review* XV, No. 4 (April 1863).

Staiger, Bruce C. "Abolitionism and the Presbyterian Schism of 1837-1838." *The Mississippi Valley Historical Review* (1949).

Stewart, J.B. *Holy Warriors: The Abolitionists and American Slavery.* Hill and Wang, 1976.

_____. *William Lloyd Garrison at Two Hundred: History, Legacy, and Memory.* Yale University Press, 2008.

Sunderland, J.T., and Brooke Herford. "The Bi-Centennial of King's Chapel, Boston." *The Unitarian: A Monthly Magazine of Liberal Christianity,* 1887.

"The Seventh Census of the United States: 1850." Robert Armstrong, Public Printer, 1853.

Thompson, G., and R. J. Breckinridge. *Discussion on American Slavery, between George Thompson: agent of the British and Foreign Society for the Abolition of Slavery throughout the world, and Robert J. Breckinridge, delegate from the General Assembly of the Presbyterian Church in the United States to the Congregational union of England and Wales: Holden in the Rev. Dr. Wardlaw's chapel, Glasgow, Scotland, on the evenings of the 13th, 14th, 15th, 16th, 17th of June, 1836.* Knapp, 1836.

_____. *Report of the Discussion on American Slavery.* D. Prentice & Co., 1836.

Thompson, Jno. R. "Slavery As A Moral Relation." *Southern Literary Messenger*, XVII, July 1851.

Thornwell, J.H. *The Rights and Duties of Masters.* Walker & James, 1850.

Tocqueville, A. *Democracy in America.* Harper Collins Publishers, 2007.

Twelve Southerners. *I'll Take My Stand: The South and the Agrarian Tradition.* Louisiana State University Press, 2006.

United States War Dept. *The War of the Rebellion: A Compilation of the Official Records of the Union and Confederate Armies.* Govt. Printing Office, 1900.

White, H.A. *Robert E. Lee and the Southern Confederacy, 1807-1870.* G. P. Putnam's Sons, 1897.

White, Ronald. *Lincoln's Greatest Speech: The Second Inaugural.* Simon & Schuster, 2006.

Williams, J., and J.B. Hopkins. *The South Vindicated.* Longman & Green, 1862.

Woods, T.E. *The Politically Incorrect Guide to American History.* Regnery, 2004.

JOSEPH JAY

Young, J.R. *Proslavery and Sectional Thought in the Early South: 1740-1829 An Anthology*. University of South Carolina Press, 2006.

About the Author

JOSEPH JAY grew up in the Northeast but frequently went on family trips to the Deep South as a boy. It was on these trips that Joseph visited Civil War battlefields and became enamored with Southern history and culture. Joseph dedicated his life to Christ at a young age and became involved in church ministry in his teenage years. After completing a bachelor of arts in history at a state school, he went on to earn a master of divinity from a Southern Baptist seminary. When not engaged in academic pursuits Joseph enjoys outdoor activities and playing music on his guitar. You can most likely find Joseph studying and sharing about the rare old times.

AVAILABLE FROM SHOTWELL

If you enjoyed this book, perhaps some of our other titles will pique your interest. The following titles are now available at Amazon and all major online retailers. Enjoy!

JOYCE BENNETT

   Maryland, My Maryland: The Cultural Cleansing of a Small Southern State

JERRY BREWER

   Dismantling the Republic

ANDREW P. CALHOUN, JR.

   My Own Darling Wife: Letters From a Confederate Volunteer [John Francis Calhoun]

JOHN CHODES

   Segregation: Federal Policy or Racism?

   Washington's KKK: The Union League During Southern Reconstruction

PAUL C. GRAHAM

   Confederaphobia: An American Epidemic

   When the Yankees Come: Former South Carolina Slaves Remember Sherman's Invasion

JAMES R. KENNEDY

   Dixie Rising: Rules for Rebels

JAMES R. & WALTER D. KENNEDY

   Punished with Poverty: The Suffering South

PHILIP LEIGH
  The Devil's Town: Hot Spring During the Gangster Era
MICHAEL MARTIN
  Southern Grit: Sensing the Siege at Petersburg
CHARLES T. PACE
  Lincoln As He Was
  Southern Independence. Why War?
JAMES RUTLEDGE ROESCH
  From Founding Fathers to Fire Eaters: The Constitutional Doctrine of States' Rights in the Old South
KIRKPATRICK SALE
  Emancipation Hell: The Tragedy Wrought By Lincoln's Emancipation Proclamation
KAREN STOKES
  A Legion of Devils: Sherman in South Carolina
  Carolina Love Letters
JOHN VINSON
  Southerner, Take Your Stand!
CLYDE N. WILSON
  Lies My Teacher Told Me: The True History of the War for Southern Independence
  SOUTHERN READER'S GUIDE
    The Old South: 50 Essential Books (I)
  THE WILSON FILES
    The Yankee Problem: An American Dilemma (1)
    Nullification: Reclaiming Consent of the Governed (2)
    Annals of the Stupid Party: Republicans Before Trump (3)

Green Altar Books (Literary Imprint)

RANDALL IVEY
  A New England Romance & Other SOUTHERN Stories

JAMES EVERETT KIBLER
  Tiller (Clay Bank County, IV)

KAREN STOKES
  Belles: A Carolina Romance
  Honor in the Dust
  The Immortals
  The Soldier's Ghost: A Tale of Charleston

GOLD-BUG (Mystery & Suspense Imprint)

MICHAEL ANDREW GRISSOM
  Billie Jo

BRANDI PERRY
  Splintered: A New Orleans Tale

MARTIN L. WILSON
  To Jekyll and Hide

FREE BOOK OFFER

Sign-up for new release notification and receive a FREE DOWNLOADABLE EDITION of Lies My Teacher Told Me: The True History of the War for Southern Independence by Dr. Clyde N. Wilson by visiting FreeLiesBook.com or by texting the word "Dixie" to 345345. You can always unsubscribe and keep the book, so you've got nothing to lose!

Southern without Apology.

www.ingramcontent.com/pod-product-compliance
Ingram Content Group UK Ltd.
Pitfield, Milton Keynes, MK11 3LW, UK
UKHW022224230426
12048UKWH00016BA/1043